# The Last Missionary

## Bob Walters

WIPF & STOCK · Eugene, Oregon

Wipf and Stock Publishers
199 W 8th Ave, Suite 3
Eugene, OR 97401

The Last Missionary
By Walters, Bob
Copyright © 2016 by Walters, Bob All rights reserved.
Softcover ISBN-13: 978-1-7252-8411-1
Hardcover ISBN-13: 978-1-7252-8410-4
eBook ISBN-13: 978-1-7252-8412-8
Publication date 10/19/2020
Previously published by Dog Ear Publishing, 2016

This edition is a scanned facsimile of the original edition published in 2016.

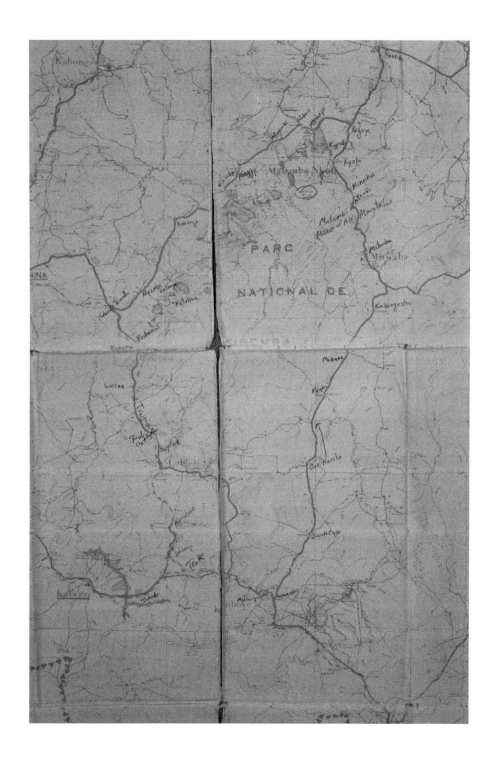

# *Forward*

$\mathcal{W}$e were together from the beginning. Starting even before I was elected bishop, on behalf of Bishop Wa Kadilo, I invited Bob to be the preacher for the North Katanga annual conference. His sermons were so well received that he was asked to preach the same series in four more conferences. When I was elected bishop, I invited Bob to come as a missionary and direct pastor training at Likasi Seminary. Those sermons and that training built the strong foundation for when the war came and pastors had to respond with courage and skill.

It was my idea that Bob bring bicycles with him to distribute to pastors. It was his idea that we buy them locally. The first year we distributed 200 bicycles. That project was our first. It made our pastors circuit riders and even today, other than a Bible, the bicycle is the most important tool for evangelism, church growth, pastoral care, and the bicycle is the village ambulance. In the villages, our pastors are known for their bicycles and Bob is famous for bringing the bicycles.

When Bob came to me with the idea of making a bicycle ride into the war zone, I thought that it was a crazy idea. He was asking to go where even I could not travel. It was not safe and I could not protect him. Reluctantly I agreed, but I put Joseph Mulongo Ndala in charge of the expedition.

Bob has lived with our people in the village, sharing their suffering. He knows more than anyone the situation of their poverty. He has been my witness. Whenever someone from America wants to know the real story, I tell them to talk with Bob. When I was receiving the Tanenbaum Peace Award in New York City, I pointed toward Bob and said, "Ask him. He has been there. He has seen it all."

Bob held up a mirror to our communities, where they can see themselves. While we appreciate all the help we are receiving from outside, Bob has forced us to look for solutions within ourselves.

What I have said to Bob, in front of his daughter, is, "Bob. People ask how to change the world. You have changed the world."

Bishop Ntambo Nkulu Ntanda
The United Methodist Church
North Katanga Episcopal Area
Democratic Republic of the Congo

*"In our end is our beginning; in our time, infinity . . ."*

—"Hymn of Promise," *The United Methodist Hymnal* #707

The manuscript of *The Last Missionary* has undergone numerous overhauls over the past several years. What started as the Reverend Dr. "Biking Bob" Walters' attempt to make his thesis accessible to the general public has morphed into an adventure story laced with challenging reflections about what he observes along the way. Far from being a book of answers, it is a book that wrestles with listening more deeply and asking better questions. It is the first in what we hope to be a series of publications on missiology.

One may rightly ask why an organization that strives to move beyond outdated models is leading with a story about a white American man serving as a missionary in the DR Congo—even telling it from his point of view. To talk about the Congo and missiology, we must have an entry point. Where better to start our conversation than at the end—the end of the era of the (neo)colonial foreign missionary.

Indeed, the day of the missionaries of lore has ended, but let us dwell together in this liminal place to discover together what is to be revealed.

The Reverend Taylor Denyer, President
Friendly Planet Missiology

# *Wafwako*

*F*irst of all, I thank Bishop Ntambo Nkulu Ntanda for a twenty-five-year friendship. As he said to my wife, Teri, "We've been together from the beginning." It has been a privilege to work for such a great peacemaker. I thank the bishop for appointing Joseph Mulongo Ndala to the Friendly Planet Missiology team. Without Mulongo, I'd be lost somewhere in the forest.

Next, I want to thank Kate Koppy for a masterful editing job, taking my gonzo-style journaling and making it a readable book. Thanks to my daughter, Taylor Denyer, for managing the whole project.

And finally, I thank my wife, Teri, for her patience and support. She has had the responsibility of a 100-year-old house, a Ford with 200,000 miles on it, and earning a paycheck teaching school, while I wandered.

Bob Walters

# Glossary

*T*his story happens within the global community known as The United Methodist Church and in a specific region of the Democratic Republic of the Congo. Here are a few words and phrases that I use that may be new to the reader.

Bukhari: Also called *fu fu* and many other names across Africa, this food staple is usually made from the flour of the cassava root. *Bukhari* can also be made from corn flour or other flours or mixtures of flours, depending upon availability and local recipes. It is served as a large lump of paste and eaten by hand; it is rolled into a small ball and dipped into a palm oil–based sauce. The meal may include chicken, fish, or goat, as well as greens.

The Congo: There are two Congos: the Republic of the Congo, sometimes referred to as Congo-Brazzaville, and the Democratic Republic of the Congo (DRC or DR Congo). We are in the Democratic Republic of the Congo. French-language news reporters in the DRC will always say the full name, "*République démocratique du Congo.*" If I just say, "the Congo," I mean either the Democratic Republic of the Congo or the Congo River.

Conductor: A church lay leader. When I first learned the word, I remarked with a laugh that *conductor* is what we call the person who runs the train. "We do, too" was the response.

Friendly Planet Missiology (FPM): A community leadership development and missiological education group led by the Reverend Taylor Denyer, the Reverend Joseph Mulongo, and the Reverend Dr. Robert Walters. FPM has offices in Mulongo, DR Congo, and Plainfield, Indiana. Visit www.friendlyplanetmissiology.org for more information.

GBGM: The General Board of Global Ministries, the missionary-sending agency of The United Methodist Church. For the record, I'm a fan of Thomas Kemper, the general secretary. The changes he is bringing to GBGM are spot-on good. However, I'm working in a gap region, where the old missionaries have gone and the new GBGM has not yet arrived.

Missiology: The study of mission systems. Our missiology is in the school of missiology coming out of the University of South Africa, where mission systems are studied from the point of view of those receiving the help. In this book we go outside of the zone of help to the villages that have not yet received and may never receive help, or that have received help in the past from missionaries, but those missionaries have left.

Missionary: I use the word *missionary* in its (neo)colonial meaning, i.e., a person coming from Europe or North America to serve in a village as a doctor, pastor, teacher, agronomist, etc. This is the way the word is understood in the villages we visit. A new generation of missionaries is being recruited from fresh talent all over the world to serve in their own communities or to go to other countries to serve, a much flatter mission model. These missionaries are the subject of a different book.

Mzungu: A Kiswahili word that functionally translates to "white person." (The plural form is *wazungu*.) *Mzungu* can be said with a range of intent, from surprise to contempt. Children in the villages call out "*Mzungu!*" with the delight of a rare sighting when I ride by. I've seen the same response when a wild monkey runs through the village. When young men call men *blanc* (French), it is always with contempt. Mostly, in the region I work, *mzungu* is simply the common identification of a white person.

Names of people: A first and last name system is not used in the Katanga region of the DRC, although some families—especially those who fly often—have started to give a common third name to their children to reduce cross-cultural confusion. When I call Mulongo *Mulongo,* I am not calling him by his last name. When I call the bishop *Bishop Ntambo,* I am not calling him by his first name. Also, individuals are often referred to by their position (e.g., bishop, pastor, conductor) rather than given names. Wives of pastors are called *mama pasteur,* so I often never learn their actual names.

Patronage: The social-economic system in which all the resources are controlled by a single person, a patron—for instance, a chief or a missionary. As a community and as individuals, clients petition the patron for needs and favors. The relationship between labor and reward is understood only in indirect ways. Honor and shame are the primary motivators.

## Introduction
## Mulongo, Katanga, DR Congo, March 2010
## I am the last missionary.

*T*here was a time when missionaries were common in the remote districts of the Democratic Republic of the Congo. They were the rescuers in an otherwise oppressive economic system. Their help kept the villagers surviving and gave them hope that someday, their struggle would reach a prosperous end. Missionaries were the link to the outside world. They had real money. They provided jobs. Oh, and yes, they preached the love of God as demonstrated in Jesus Christ to a hungry people in an inhospitable land.

Missionaries were the referees of the constant wrestling for position in a world that is both postcolonial and neocolonial. They buffered the jealousies that fed the village gossip. And for a young person who wanted more out of life, a relationship with the missionary was the way out of the village.

Brave and compassionate, they came to save souls and make life better. They came into a system they could not control and did not understand, a system that could not deliver what it promised. Just as unaware of their function as the people they came to serve, missionaries were the priests of a patronage system that rescued the community from its poverty and, at the same time, ensured that the community would never become self-sufficient.

Here's the thing: The missionaries, then and now, think that they are proclaiming a simple and straightforward Gospel message aimed at converting the hearts of natives to Jesus Christ, fully unaware that those to whom they are preaching live in a world more like the world of Jesus than the missionary can ever know. The ones being preached to bring the missionary into their world to play the role of the patron in an economic system that they intuitively understand better than the one preaching. Unwittingly, the missionary reinforces the very problem that the Gospel is meant to remedy.

Armed with the best of social science and systems theories, I set out in 1997, as a United Methodist missionary, to do theological battle with this patronage system. I came to the Congo with the passion of Jesus driving the money changers out of the Temple. If St. Patrick could drive the snakes out of Ireland, I could drive the missionaries out of the Congo.

I must confess that I was filled with a righteous anger.

I imagined God saying, "Last one out, close the door." And I intended to be that last one out.

But that's not how it happened. I didn't drive out the missionaries. The war in eastern Congo, however, did.

My career as a missionary was over before it began, lasting just a few short months. In August 1998 the General Board of Global Ministries (GBGM) in New York decided to evacuate all United Methodist missionaries from the Democratic Republic of the Congo. With my bicycle, two live goats, and a 6-foot stalk of bananas strapped to the roof, I drove the Land Cruiser out of the mountains of the Mitwaba District and three days later joined the caravan of departing missionaries in Lubumbashi. When we crossed the border into Zambia at Kasumbalesa, I believed that I would never return.

In the years that followed, eastern Congo fell into a horrific war. Villages were burned, some more than once. Rape and machete were the weapons of choice, which made this war especially terrifying to villagers. While America was reeling from 9/11, millions of Congolese were dying. Few outside of the Congo took note.

There was, however, a good news story in the midst of the horror.

When the missionaries left, the Congolese leadership of The United Methodist Church stepped up. One such leader was Bishop Ntambo Nkulu, who decided that he would not run away and that The United Methodist Church in North Katanga would remain in place. More than that, Bishop Ntambo and his pastors continued to build churches, schools, and clinics. While everyone else was fleeing for their lives, they stood fast. Bishop Ntambo provided the only alternative vision to the chaos and hopelessness of the war. Bishop Ntambo brokered local peace accords with warlords and with the government's army. The war was stopped 40 kilometers outside Kamina, a key up-country crossroads and the center of the North Katanga Conference of The United Methodist Church.

This steadfastness was not without cost. Pastors and lay leaders, sent by the bishop, advanced into the war zone to serve communities there. Many gave their lives. Those who didn't give their lives gave their livelihoods. They went with nothing to villages that had nothing to give to them, poverty serving poverty, suffering serving suffering.

The Congolese United Methodists knew the secrets of community development and of peace building. When everyone else panicked, they maintained a steady course. When all the others were crying for help, they were the incarnation of help. The United Methodist Church in Katanga grew dramatically in numbers and in reputation, becoming the church that people trusted.

Another such leader was Pastor Jackie Mwayuma, who serves the Kabalo District. Kabalo was occupied by several different armies during the eight-year war in eastern Congo (1998–2006). The railroad crosses the Congo River at Kabalo. The armies of Rwanda and Uganda approached the bridge from the east side of the river, while the armies of Zimbabwe and the DRC came from the west. As they pushed one another back and forth across the river for control of the bridge, the villages nearby were overrun and burned, some as many as four times.

Rape was the lead weapon of this war, and it effectively traumatized everyone involved. Soldiers raped women in the streets in a brutal and public display of violence, then left them there as thrown-away garbage. The rapes were meant to humiliate the husbands and fathers of the village, to render the men of the village powerless. Any resistance was met with machetes. It wasn't sufficient to kill an opponent with a bullet. This was a war of total terror. These villagers weren't combatants. They were innocent residents, in the way.

Public brutality was also a lesson aimed at the soldiers yet reluctant to engage in rape. Not that I would want to compare their forced participation to the trauma experienced by the young women, but the young men in the armies were traumatized in these rapes. To be a soldier was to be a rapist, and many would come to find a rush of ferocity in the act. Others were destroyed emotionally.

In addition to the public rape of women as an act of conquest, there was the taking of young women—young teenagers and preteens—as wives for the invading soldiers. The young women would be kept for up to two years. When the soldiers moved on or retreated, they were left behind with their babies conceived in rape.

This is why Jackie was sent to Kabalo. The bishop had sent her to pastor the people and to help rebuild the community. She had received special training in post-trauma counseling at Africa University in Zimbabwe and was deemed uniquely qualified for the task.

She arrived with nothing. Her household goods were stolen on the long journey from Kamina to Kabalo. And the community there had nothing to offer her.

It seemed to me that someone needed to go to Kabalo to see Jackie and make certain she was OK. It was going to take me four years to get there.

I've structured the telling of this story on the model of Robert Pirsig's *Zen and the Art of Motorcycle Maintenance:* personal travelogue interspersed with reflections on missiology.

Like Pirsig, I'm writing right on the edge of crazy. This, it seems, may not have been an uncommon condition for a solo white explorer in Africa. Maybe it's the heat and the fever, maybe it's the feeling of isolation in the middle of so many people. Maybe it's that it just takes a certain kind of crazy to enjoy this kind of adventure. Maybe it is being so out of step with one's own culture and out of touch with this one. Maybe it's expecting to arrive at the end of the universe and finding instead a whole world of people who are, on one hand, familiar, and on the other hand, so incredibly different. Maybe for me, it is the conflict of hating the idea of being a white missionary in Africa and the irresistible call to be here. Nonetheless, I invite you to go deep into the *Heart of Darkness* and allow the crazy to take charge.

If you think this book will lay out a clear and logical plan for the redevelopment of a broken part of the world, you'll be disappointed. Like Pirsig, I put forth ideas that are counterlogical, countercultural, and counterintuitive. The conventional wisdom is not working. The people running this world have given the people of southeastern Congo nothing but misery. Something has to change. The Congolese look forward to change; they pray for change. They look to their government for change. They look to missionaries for change. They look to Barack Obama for change. They look to God for change. But they get more of the same. The same misery. All day. Every day. The same.

When things have gone so wrong, everything must be challenged: every idea, every custom, every teaching by missionaries, every truth. The bad stuff didn't cause the present condition. The bad stuff moved into the void created when the good stuff stopped working. We must challenge the good practices, too. Even the foundations of our faith must be challenged. Before I can say to a people that Jesus is the answer, I must be willing to first entertain the possibility that he is not.

It is 2010. I'm back in the Democratic Republic of the Congo. A missionary, once more. No contract. No mission board paying me. I'm just here following a call that I cannot name. I am a missionary again, on an adventure that was, two years ago, only a dream, an impossible dream.

A few good friends have convinced me to tell this story. It is a very good story, an important story. It's a story of people who struggle to maintain life and livelihood in small remote villages in the mountains and along the rivers of Katanga. A story of the church and its mission, what it has been and what it could be. A story of how the global community treats the smallest village in Africa and how that has an effect on all of us.

I'll try to tell you the story as I take a long bicycle ride with a few Congolese friends to visit remote districts who haven't received a pastoral visit since the war ended in 2006. It's a ride of 1,000 kilometers, so there is plenty of time to reflect. Be patient.

My mind is undisciplined in writing and I think I'm running a fever from an infection in my leg. I hope my reflections resonate with you, reader.

In the end, this story is about local community leaders, like Pastor Joseph Mulongo, who are doing exactly what The United Methodist Church has asked them to do. Unfortunately, they are doing it without support. While Americans are getting caught up in huge, celebrity-led, donor-driven fund-raising campaigns to save Africa, talented and courageous community leaders are dying. If this story has a point, it is that there are leaders in place in the villages of Katanga who are ready and able to move their communities forward, given just a bit of attention and help.

There will be no Land Cruiser this time. My bike is all I'll have. Ride with the madman on a bicycle and see where this takes us.

# The Cannondale T1,
## The Land Rover Defender of Bicycles
### Indiana, 2009

One look at the Michelin map taught me that it would be impossible for a solo cyclist to ride a bicycle all the way up to Kabalo from Lubumbashi. The roads were impassable with no bridges where bridges had to be, and no one could say whether those same roads were safe from armed militia. It was not at all possible and not at all safe. No one in the Congolese government would give me the necessary travel documents to enter this area.

So I came up with the substitute idea that I'd make a practice run of 1,000 kilometers in a loop around the districts south of Kabalo. I could travel on mission documents created by The United Methodist Church. If that worked out, I could make an attempt to reach Kabalo the second year. I pitched the idea to Bishop Ntambo, who was not immediately thrilled. He saw it as too dangerous and just not something that made any sense to him. What would be the purpose? How would I eat? Where was safe drinking water? Where would I sleep? Even he could not visit these districts because of the security risks. Reluctantly he agreed to the trip, if I would agree to travel with a small group of pastors he would select for my security.

Shortly after the bishop agreed, I received an e-mail from Joseph Mulongo stating that he would be traveling with me the whole trip. In my imagining of the trip, I had seen a rolling plan where I would pick up a team as I entered a district and drop it at the exit, picking up a fresh team through the next district. I wouldn't have thought to inconvenience anyone by asking them to go the distance with me.

The preparations began in earnest. I ordered a Cannondale T1 touring bike from Bicycle Garage Indy (BGI). This was my dream bike, the Land Rover Defender of bicycles, and it even comes in Land Rover Defender white. The factory makes this particular model only on a short run once a year in December. The window for receiving the bicycle and getting it through shakedown was tiny.

Several calls to the factory alerted us that my bike was delayed for lack of the wheels sourced for the T1. We asked them to break their own factory rules and ship the bicycle to BGI without the wheels. Frank, the mechanic at BGI, built me a custom set of wheels at no extra cost. He also took me through the whole bike, bit by bit, as he built it, and provided all the spare parts he could imagine my needing on the road, including a ziplock bag full of bolts, cables, presized spokes, chain sections, and the coolest multitool. The best thing Frank did for me was select a BMX pedal set to replace the standard touring pedals.

British Airways allowed me three checked bags, a generous allowance. I was coming with the missionary class ticket, the lowest BA class in coach, but with the first class baggage allowance. The bike was packed into an airline bicycle case, and the racks, panniers, and camping equipment went into a second hard case. My third bag carried stuff for the team, two laptop computers for a professor at Mulungwishi Seminary, and a propeller governor for the United Methodist aviation program. All my personal clothing was in my backpack carry-on.

*London*
*January 2010*

Brought by Faithful hands
over Land and Sea
Here Rests
DAVID LIVINGSTONE,
Missionary,
Traveller,
Philanthropist,
Born March 19, 1813,
AT BLANTYRE, LANARKSHIRE,
Died May 1, 1873,
AT CHITAMBO'S VILLAGE, ULALA.
For 30 years his life was spent
in an unwearied effort
to evangelize the native races,
to explore the undiscovered secrets,
to abolish the desolating slave trade,
of CENTRAL AFRICA,
where with his last words he wrote,
"All I can add in my solitude, is,
may heaven's rich blessing come down
on everyone, American, English, or Turk,
who will help to heal
this open sore of the world."

$\mathcal{M}$y favorite route to the DR Congo is British Airways to London, London to Lusaka. Since 1991, I've made this crossing maybe a dozen times. In the 1990s it meant a packed Boeing 747, sitting in the back of the plane on that missionary class ticket. In my former life in the navy, we called this just forward of steerage.

Back in the day, BA offered British TV shows, *Mr. Bean* and *Absolutely Fabulous,* and whatever movie Hugh Grant was in that week. I read big books like John Dominic Crossan's *The Historical Jesus,* Peter Senge's *The Fifth Discipline,* and Jared Diamond's *Guns, Germs, and Steel.*

In January 2010, I retrace my old route, but this time in a more comfortable 777 with an individual entertainment screen with too many choices. I find an old Hugh Grant movie to watch and read Erhard Gerstenberger's *Theologies in the Old Testament.*

In London, routinely, I would go to Westminster Abbey to see David Livingstone. If it was not Sunday, I'd stop in at Harrods to buy my wife, Teri, a gift, and if it was not Saturday night, I'd have lunch at the Hard Rock Cafe. It was also the last chance for a Big Mac and fries at McDonald's. Don't hate.

This time London is cool and foggy. It is not great weather, but it is comfortable enough. Riding the Underground into the city feels so familiar, as if I am simply a commuter off to work. I have enough time to give the Abbey a long visit, but not enough to do anything else. At the airport I had exchanged a $50 bill for pounds sterling. That is enough for the tube ticket, the £15 entrance fee for the Abbey, and lunch.

All the other tourists in the Abbey seem to be listening to a recorded tour on rented headsets and looking up. I look up. The room is impressive, too much to take in. I have no idea what they're being told. I look down at the markers on the floor, and am delighted when I see names I recognize: Wilberforce, Gladstone, Captain Cooke. I walk slowly, reverently, prayerfully. There is an order to the parade of visitors, like walking a labyrinth. Mostly I stay in line and am careful not to disturb others, but they are interested in royalty, stopping frequently at the ornate tombs. I'm interested in the more common folk who happened to make some nearly forgotten mark in history. Their small plaques are in the niches or on the floor. No need to rush, though. By following the given order, I'll find David Livingstone at the end of the tour. Before the nave, there's Poets' Corner with a new find for me: Rudyard Kipling. As a prayer, I repeat the lines of "If" that I can remember: "If you can meet with Triumph and Disaster and treat those two impostors just the same. . ." or something like that.

Finally, I find him where I left him last. On the marble floor, in the middle of the nave, among the lesser heroes who got there by some curious act of Parliament when the Church and the Crown weren't paying attention, there he is: David Livingstone, Missionary, Traveler, Philanthropist. I've also visited his heart, buried in Chitambo's Village in what is now Zambia.

Why do I keep coming here? Here is the prototype of the colonial missionary. I tell myself that I should hate him and the movement he represents, but I'm drawn to him. There is a connection. I must learn what that is. The secret to understanding my call is somehow in this African explorer-missionary.

The tour is over.

Before leaving the Abbey, I light a couple of candles: one for Teri's dad, the other for pastors in the Congo.

I walk out the front doors of the Abbey and turn to see the 20th Century Martyrs, King, Romero, and Bonhoeffer among them. I was here on that day twelve years ago when these statues were unveiled.

Then I give up my last pounds sterling for a hot dog and a Coke from a rolling stand on the street. Money well spent.

# Lusaka, Zambia

*F*ifteen minutes from landing in Lusaka, the sun is coming up. We're still at 37,000 feet, and the cloud layer looks to be at about 25,000. To the east, bright oranges and blue-grays paint the black-and-white world in stripes. Out of the west side of the plane, the light is slowly overtaking the darkness in shades of blue, white, and gray. The day is dawning, and I've moved from cold, wintry Indiana to hot, rainy Zambia. Like the Underground in London, the tarmac at the Lusaka airport is familiar. The heat and humidity are familiar. The routine of customs and immigration is familiar.

All my checked luggage made the trip, but my bags come onto the baggage conveyer belt last. That wait just kills me, worrying that a bag might not have made a plane change along the way. Yes, I'm a seasoned traveler and love to fly, but I'm still an anxious traveler, never able to shake the fear that I've forgotten something important, or lost my passport, or whatever.

The oversized bicycle case came in through a separate door and is over against the wall by itself. All my bags had been opened and searched by the American TSA and British Airways, with stickers on the outside and notices inside. But they are there with their contents: the Cannondale, the racks and panniers, the laptops, and the prop governor. A sigh of relief.

My daughter, Taylor, a United Methodist pastor, and her husband, Stuart, the vice-consul at the U.S. Embassy in Lusaka, pick me up at the airport. In Zambia, Stuart's diplomatic credentials give him access beyond the security points, and I enjoy the quick pass through immigration.

The weekend in Lusaka with Taylor and Stuart is spent on a Saturday visit to an environmental park and Sunday attendance at a church in the township of Matero, a new congregation meeting in a school classroom in a slum. As worship begins, the pastor asks if I could preach. This is not unusual in Africa, and as Mr. Wesley ordered his preachers, "Be prepared to preach, pray, or die at a moment's notice," I am ready.

I preach on my go-to text, Revelation 2:8–11: "I know of your poverty, but you are rich!" I tell the duck story I ripped off Kierkegaard, and eight young adults respond by coming forward for a special blessing. I lay hands on each of them as I plead with God for something good to happen in their young lives.

## Crossing the Border at Kasumbalesa

*M*onday, we meet up with Jeff and Ellen Hoover, missionaries in Lubumbashi, who were in Lusaka to meet David and Lori Persons, missionaries to Mulungwishi just arriving from the States, and they offer me a ride to Lubumbashi. Having no other plan, I take them up on the offer.

We overnight with Delbert and Sandy Groves in Kitwe and drop off some luggage at John Enright's in Ndola. Without having planned to do so, I manage to run into several missionaries on my way through the Copperbelt region of northern Zambia.

A few times over the years, I've had the pleasure of dining at the Greek Club in Lubumbashi with the Hoovers and the Persons, and others. Jeff knows the hundred-year history of United Methodists in the Congo. He is one of the smartest people I know. Both Jeff and Ellen have PhDs from Yale.

Both Lori and David are second-generation missionaries. They grew up here. Lori's father was one of the early missionaries pushing for black leadership of the church. The Methodists were the minority voice on this issue. When a national council of Protestant churches was formed, Lori's father was the Methodist delegate. The reserve delegate was black. Lori's father feigned sickness in order to excuse himself and seat the reserve. That was not taken well by the heads of the other denominations, all white.

This is to say, that before I get too far down the road on my antimissionary story, that there are many truly great missionary stories.

What I'm dealing with is not whether missionaries have been good or bad, but this question: Why is it not working?

We cross the border at Kasumbalesa. The crossing goes without major incident. Jeff is an old pro.

What is overwhelming at the border now is the number of transports. Huge double-trailer tractor-trailers crowd the road for ten kilometers either side. Cars snake their way through the parked lines of trucks. These trucks can wait for weeks to clear customs. Goods of all kinds are moving from South Africa into the DRC through Zambia.

Mud. It's all a mud parking lot. There is no official order, but local youth appoint themselves as traffic managers expecting tips for their services, asking for $20, maybe getting 500 Congo francs (50 cents).

The road from the border to Lubumbashi is all new blacktop, Chinese built. Along the way, Jeff complains that the signs for towns are all misspelled. Jeff picks up a police officer at the border who has asked for a ride to Lubumbashi. The posted speed limit along this new road is 40 kilometers per hour. Jeff was stopped and ticketed last trip, so this time he obeys the speed limit. The police officer asks why he is driving so slowly. Probably the speed limit is meant to be 40 kilometers per hour through towns and higher on the open road, but the signage is so confusing, the enforcement so random, and the fines so high, $300, that Jeff just feels he can't risk it.

## Lubumbashi, Democratic Republic of the Congo

*I* have grown to hate Lubumbashi.

Not like my wife hates it.

Teri hates it for its rudeness. In the villages, people are polite. Hospitality is the rule. In Lubumbashi young women in blue jeans make contemptuous remarks to her face.

And not like our daughter hates it.

Taylor hates it because it is noisy and dangerous with traffic. Even we can remember when there were few cars and the town was quiet. It's also expensive. Room and board can eat up all your reserves as you wait for the train or plane to Kamina.

I hate Lubumbashi for what it means to the young adults trying to get ahead. People are flocking to the city from the villages with dreams of making big money. Once they are in the city, though, they find that renting a place to live is beyond their means: $50 a month for a small room with a dirt floor in a slum. No money for transportation. No paying jobs. School fees they can't afford. The system of relatives that sustains them in the village becomes the system of relatives that scams them in the city.

On the positive side, there are plenty of friends in town, and I can usually find them downtown at the Methodist Center, an office building that houses both the Southern Congo Conference offices and the dislocated offices for the North Katanga Conference. Although the conference center for North Katanga is in Kamina, the lack of a working banking system in North Katanga in 2010 means that an office in Lubumbashi continues to be necessary.

At the Methodist Center, it is a treat to be greeted by Mama Louise, a ninety-year-old Swiss missionary who is content to finish her days in Lubumbashi. She hangs out at the restaurant there and, even at ninety, is pretty spry. Teri and I remember her from the road trip that we all shared with Ntambo, driving from Kolwezi to Lubumbashi back in 1996. She was old then and thought that that trip would be her last up-country. A few years back, she tried to retire and moved in with her sister in Switzerland. Within months she was back in Lubumbashi. She'll die here.

I want to spend as little time as possible in Lubumbashi. My Congolese colleagues and I are not on the same page on this and don't seem to appreciate how anxious I am to get to out of this city. Taylor and I have declared Tenke to be our base of operations. It is accessible by road from Lubumbashi. The hospitality there is good. We stay in the home of the district superintendent, a house built with money provided by churches in Indiana. There is electricity and a nearby cell tower. There's no running water, but the outhouse has a cement floor and is always clean.

I must wait for travel documents. In the DRC you must travel with your passport and a document from immigration that states your whole itinerary. If a town is not on the document, you don't go there. Getting this paper may take several days.

I check in at the Methodist Guest House across the street from the Jerusalem United Methodist Church. The guest house represents my internal struggle with being a white missionary. On the plus side, it is safe and comfortable, with electricity (most of the time), American-style bathrooms with running water, even hot water for a shower or tub bath. Nothing fancy, but comfortable for the traveler. Mama Odia, who has managed the house since before anyone's memory, is delightful and always seems genuinely happy that I'm here.

The big negative for me around the guest house is its missionary history. When I came the first time back in 1991, this was a missionary guest house—for missionaries, by missionaries. No local Congolese church leaders were allowed. It smelled a bit of apartheid. The guest house represented the divide between missionaries and the Congolese church. When Teri and I were there in 1996, we innocently invited our friend Ntambo, now Bishop Ntambo, to stay with us. He graciously declined, knowing that he was not welcome in the guest house.

On the practical side, the $35 a night is a bit steep for me, and there are no meals provided except fixings for instant coffee. The backup is the Catholic guest house, where I'm also well received and have an ongoing personal relationship with the staff, but the cost there is $60 per night, but with meals included. Okay, $35 per night is a bargain compared to the $300 a night at the Grand Karavia or $100 a night at the Park Hotel, but I'm on a tight budget and thus need to get out of town fast.

Despite my theoretical disdain of the Methodist Guest House, I feel at home here. Mama Odia greets me as if I were her favorite guest of all time. She asks about Taylor, "How's she doing?" She gives me my favorite room.

I settle into my room, set up my laptop and take advantage of the electricity. There's not enough electricity in the grid to power every neighborhood at once, so Lubumbashi has rolling blackouts. It is wise to charge everything that needs charging while you have a chance. I write a bit on a book that I've been struggling with for several years now. Right now it has the working title of *Saints under the Altar*, a reference to Revelation 6:9. It's an attempt to make my doctoral thesis readable.

# *Shabana*

*I* have no plan yet, except for the idea that I want to ride my bicycle a total of at least 1,000 kilometers into some remote districts. At this point I am completely clueless as to what I would find, how I would survive, and who would go with me. I don't even know the why. Joseph Mulongo had said that he would meet me in Tenke and ride with me the whole way. I had just settled in at the guesthouse when Shabana shows up. He brings his brother Prospère. I had not really asked them to go with me, but when they show up, the core team is created. Shabana, a young man in his twenties and the son of a pastor, is a friend of Taylor's from her time in Kamina in 2005. He had heard through her that I am taking this trip. Shabana has a degree in English from the teachers college, so I am thinking that he can be my translator and language coach. Prospère speaks less English than I speak French, so he just sits and smiles. I like him instantly. Something about that smile.

I offer Shabana and his brother soft drinks from the stash of Coke and Fanta that Mama Odia keeps in the guest house refrigerator, a way of augmenting her income.

We sit drinking our Fantas and planning the trip. First thing is to get ourselves to Tenke, where we would meet up with Mulongo. We need to find bicycles for Prospère, Shabana, and Mulongo. Tomorrow we would shop for bikes and find a way to Tenke.

I give each of them a $100 bill as an advance so that they can buy what they need for the trip. Prospère is delighted, but Shabana asks if I can pay him the full amount I was planning to pay him so that he can settle his debts before leaving town. I agree and give him four more $100 bills.

# Taqwa to Tenke

$\mathcal{T}$ he next day—I don't even know what day it is—Shabana and Prospère
arrive around 10:00 a.m., and we go shopping. In the bustling downtown
we find the Taqwa bus company. The bus for Kolwezi leaves every morning at 8:00
a.m. sharp. We buy three tickets for tomorrow's bus, $50 each.

Next we find a shop that sells bikes. The bikes we want—made in India, brand
name Kinga, model 4x4 (*quatre pour quatre*)—are $100 each and come in a box of
four. For ease of handling, and in case we pick up another rider, we buy the box of
four bicycles. The bicycles, however, are at the warehouse and we have to come
back for them in about an hour or so.

Shabana has errands to run, so we agree that I'll go back to the guesthouse to get
my bicycle, and we will meet at the bus office at 4:00 p.m. to arrange for the bikes
to travel as cargo to Tenke. I had originally thought that I would assemble my bike
in Lubumbashi and ride to Tenke, a two-day ride, but the road to Tenke is busy
with heavy trucks that make riding a bicycle a life-risking exercise.

We get the box of new bikes and my bicycle case to the Taqwa shipping office, a
hole-in-the-wall on a busy side street, just before it closes for the day. We pay for
their transport, another $50 for each case, wrap them in packing tape, and leave
them to be preloaded as freight on the bus. The bus goes all the way to Kolwezi, but
we'll get off at Tenke. Our bikes are well marked to get off at Tenke.

The next morning Shabana, Prospère, and I board the bus to Tenke. Forget what
you might have heard about Africa Time; this bus departs promptly at 8:00 a.m.
The Taqwa bus has assigned seats, one to a seat, except for small children who sit
on laps or in the aisle. The interior is a bit worn but not uncomfortable. It is covered in road dust, inside and out. This bus began life in South Africa as a high-end
tour bus. The Congo gets South Africa's hand-me-downs.

It's customary in the DR Congo to have church on the bus as it leaves town. On this
ride, a Pentecostal preacher leads us in singing, reads scripture, preaches, takes an offering, then gets off at the edge of town. Actually, it is not a bad sermon, as near as my lim-
ited language skills can determine, and everybody on board appreciates it.

I settle in for the long bus ride, taking full advantage of my window seat. Two advantages: I can watch this wonderful world go by, and I can open the window for air. I long ago left the world of air conditioning, but it's not too hot, if I can find a breeze.

About an hour out of Lubumbashi, the toll road begins. A Chinese construction company is just starting the work of repaving. The toll plaza looks more like the entrance to an industrial area than an interstate highway. Tolls are high: $100 for a commercial truck. Yes, it does seem like $100 is the cost of everything. U.S. $100 bills are the currency franca for business in this poverty-stricken country.

The big trucks are carrying heavy machines and goods to the mines or coming from the mines loaded with copper or cobalt. Midsized trucks carry goods for the towns along the road. Some of the smaller trucks will turn north at Lwamba for Mitwaba and Mulongo.

Minibuses are packed full of people. I used to ride the minibus from Likasi to Lubumbashi and back, back in the day. As a *mzungu,* I was usually given the best seat on the hump between the driver's seat and the front passenger seat, with my nose against the windscreen. It was a dangerous way to travel back then, and it's only gotten worse. On a bus ride back from Tenke last year, Taylor and I witnessed the aftermath of a minibus-truck accident. The dead, dozens of them, were laid out in ranks and rows awaiting the single ambulance that was on its way from Lubumbashi. The scene was too gruesome to feel real. Taylor made me promise to never ride the minibus again.

After six hours and a handful of stops, including Likasi, where I had lived as a missionary in the 1990s, we arrive at the bus stop for Tenke. Actually, the town of Tenke is another seven kilometers off the road. The stop is a small strip of makeshift shops on the side of the road.

We are met by Boy Scouts who load our luggage, including bicycles, onto their bikes and lead us toward town. We follow on the footpath. It's all whistles and marching and singing. Eventually, the scouts break ranks and move out at their own accelerated pace, disappearing into the forest.

About halfway to town, we are met by the United Methodist Women, singing and dancing in uniform (yellow head scarves, green blouses, and *kikwembe* skirts in the United Methodist print). It's singing and dancing the rest of the way in.

# Tenke, 2010

*T*he Tenke parsonage is new construction, built with money raised by Bishop Ntambo on his tours of Indiana, Ohio, and Texas. It is the model parsonage in his vision for The United Methodist Church in North Katanga. Basic in design, the parsonage is a brick three-bedroom home, with a single-pitch metal roof, a skim coat of cement for finish, and steel doors for security. There is no running water, and no finished ceiling inside. The toilet is outside, but there is a bathing room inside, a small room with a hole in the wall at the floor to drain water to the outside gutter. Because it is close to the railroad, this house has electricity, most of the time.

Inside are two couches and two matching chairs around a low table for the living/dining room and a small dining table. In the States, the furniture would look like an assortment of Goodwill rejects and some tables out of the barn, but here it looks good. This parsonage has a TV/VCR/DVD set for entertainment. There is now a broadcast channel with news, Nigerian serials, football matches, Christian music videos produced in Kinshasa or Tanzania, and commercials. Phone and laptop chargers are plugged in all the time. On Sunday mornings, young men are busy ironing their dress shirts with the electric iron. The newest thing for a well-equipped home is a freezer. The electricity is too undependable for a refrigerator, but a freezer works well because the frozen food can coast through power outages. A little cash is made on the side in the ice business. Mostly jugs of ice are kept in the freezer.

In the main room of the house, the small dining table is filled with pots and pans of food. *Bukari* in an insulated food carrier with a screw-on lid is the centerpiece, like a Thermos bottle, only much wider for food. It has a picnic sort of design with the theme name *Hopeness,* an obvious Chinese to English translation, which is not incorrect, but not quite right.

The *bukhari* is fresh and hot. There are a bowl of chicken, a bowl of fish, a bowl of goat meat, a bowl of rice, a bowl of beans, two bowls of greens, a bowl of tomato and palm oil sauce, a small traditional wooden cup of diced hot peppers called *peri peri,* and some peanuts. The pastor's wife comes to the living room where we are seated and curtsies, saying "*Karibu kwa mesa,*" which means "Welcome to table." She then disappears to the outdoor kitchen with the other women.

When it is not raining, cooking is done out of doors with multiple generations of women working together. This is where you will find the women and small children most of the time. When it rains, cooking moves into the kitchen, a small building just behind the back door. There is no stove or cabinetry or furnishings of any kind—just small portable charcoal fire boxes and dozens of pots and bowls.

We go to the table, but first we must wash our hands. A pitcher, a bowl, a bar of soap, and a towel are on a chair waiting for us. I'm invited to go first. My host pours water over my hands into the bowl. I wash my hands with the soap, rinse, and dry them on the towel. This ritual is never skipped, even when we are on the road. It does serve for disease control as we will use our hands to eat, but there is something spiritual about it as well. It reminds me of Jesus's washing the disciples' feet before the meal. There is a social order to the ritual: The most important guest goes first, and women serve men. On the other hand, it is not unusual to see the order broken intentionally to demonstrate an awareness of the Gospel lesson that the first will go last and the last first.

District superintendent Daniel Mumba Masimono and his family are our gracious hosts. Theirs is a happy enough family with enough prosperity to live relatively well. Whatever struggles they're dealing with at the moment are carefully hidden from me. They are poor compared to American families, even those below the poverty line, but they are a leading family in Tenke, so they host important guests like us. It is customary for this hosting to far outspend what is given in return. I try not to overburden the family, but direct payment for hospitality is not accepted. Sometime during the visit, I'll meet with Mumba privately and give him an envelope with a couple $100 bills in it.

The master bedroom, the room with the only real bed, is mine. My hosts, with their youngest baby, will move into one of the children's bedrooms to sleep on a foam mattress on the floor. The children are farmed out to extended family. The rest of the team is scattered throughout the village. It is a mystery to me where they sleep, but I'm practicing the discipline of not asking.

Let me pause the story to say a bit about hospitality norms. Hospitality seems to trump all other obligations. There is great social pressure to house and feed the visitor. Hospitality and health care keep families broke. On top of this, there is an assumption that *wazungu* require a higher level of hospitality. However, in my travels, I have been caught in places where the community's best was sharing a bamboo mat on the dirt floor of a grass-roofed hut. I can guess that the others in the team have crashed with relatives or rolled out a mat in the corner of an outbuilding. Even though I'm cool with whatever is offered, it would be shaming (at this point in our relationship) to inquire of the others.

Our mechanic, Éléphant, whom I take an instant liking to, has already taken over the front porch and has unboxed the four Kingas and is busy building them. It's organized chaos with parts for four different bicycles dumped out all in one pile. These bikes have to be built from scratch. On the concrete floor there are spokes, ball bearings, everything down to the very smallest of pieces that make up a bicycle. While Éléphant builds the bicycles, my mind drifts into internal storytelling.

## Tenke, 1998

$\mathcal{T}$he first time I visited Tenke was back in 1998. I was on my first district bicycle tour, and Tenke was where I finished.

We were deep in the Lubudi District when the district conductor (lay leader) and I decided that in order to make our Sunday appointment at Tenke, we were going to have to leave the rest of our team and strike out across the mountain on our own. Pushing our loaded bikes up the mountain, through high grass, on trails that frequently disappeared, we quickly ran out of food and water. He spoke no English and I spoke no Kiluba. We made a comical pair.

This is where I began to develop a faith walk that trusts my personal survival to the ones I came to help. I was days from my comfort zone, without food or water, unable to speak the language, dependent upon someone I had met just the previous week, lost in a jungle on the other side of the world from my home in Indiana, in the middle of who knows where, suffering heat with a humidity to match, and the mountain goes straight up. I've never been so spent and so lost, and yet I've never been so centered and at one with the universe.

In a mountain village, far off the beaten path, the conductor found a relative who fixed us a meal: a tin of sardines, *peri peri* (hot peppers), and, of course, *bukari*. The second night we stayed in a small hut in a strange village and had no meal except an ear of roasted corn for breakfast. The third day we drank water from a roadside stream that I strained through my handkerchief and ate a cucumber that the conductor had purchased from the only farmer we saw on the road that day.

After three days lost—I was lost; he was not—we came upon a town I recognized, the mining town of Fungarume. I knew that there was a huge market in Fungarume, a place where one could buy a Coke, and I knew that Fungarume was just 10 kilometers from Tenke. It was close to sunset, so we labored on, passing on the Coke, even trying to pick up the pace. Ten kilometers is so seductive. It sounds so close.

The sun was down on Sunday evening when we pulled into Tenke. We had missed our Sunday morning appointment to preach by a full day. Our arrival one whole day late was a deep disappointment to the community. This disappointment did not deter their hospitality, though. In 1998, the new Tenke church building, which had been started seventeen years before and then stalled, was only a foundation, and the congregation worshipped in a too small grass-roofed building that was in pretty sorry shape. The parsonage was also in a sorry state, but as a guest, I was given the bedroom with the only bed (antique iron frame, noisy springs), a tiny window with rough wooden shutters and no glass, and a leaking roof. It was raining.

The fever hit me. Probably malaria, but maybe something else. Lord knows that I had been exposed to everything. I recalled drinking water from a roadside ditch. In the moment, I hoped it was malaria, because cholera is not a good alternative. The next three days were the sickest days of my life: fever, sweats, chills, vomiting, diarrhea. I never thought that I was going to die, but I sure did wish that I would. No one stepped up to care for me. I was left alone. Maybe this kind of sick was so much the norm that no one reacted to it, or maybe because I was *mzungu,* no one knew what to do for me. I had noticed that when Ntambo announced that he had malaria, he disappeared for a couple of days. That seems to be how it's done.

By the third day, I was able to drink some hot tea and eat a little bread. I had survived. I walked to the market, weak but upright, and bought a can of powdered milk and Nesquik. So this is what you do when you have malaria: You ride it out. If you are strong and healthy, you make it. If not, you die. I'm remembering the story of David Livingstone and how he died of blackwater fever. Was I slightly suicidal back then? Perhaps. But I truly wanted to go as deep into the experience as I could imagine.

Shortly after that first visit to Tenke in 1998, I met with Bishop Ntambo, he released construction funds, and the new church and parsonage in Tenke were finished. Mostly, that is—the church still has an unfinished look to it, with even scaffolding still in place.

While the others on the team were probably only humoring a crazy missionary, the conductor who rode with me across the mountains understood what I was trying to do. After our trip, he continued the practice of visiting all the parishes annually in the Lubudi District, then in the Tenke District when it was formed. When I met him again ten years later, he could tell me the names of all the villages he and I had visited. He reveled in retelling our story and then sternly scolded the district superintendent for allowing the practice to discontinue in the Lubudi District.

It seems fitting that the 2010 team's adventure begins in Tenke, where my earlier adventure ended.

# Tenke to Mulungwishi

*W*hen our 2010 team leaves Tenke, there is an excitement about launching this expedition. Joseph Mulongo had left the day before on the bus for Mulungwishi. Shabana, Prospère, Éléphant, and I would ride.

The morning air is crisp, and our legs are fresh. Mornings can be relatively cool and damp with a lot of moisture in the air. It's jacket weather for my Congolese colleagues, but still T-shirt weather for me. We make a few last-minute adjustments to the bikes we had packed the night before. There's a filling breakfast of coffee and bread. Team photos are taken. Then we kick off, slowly negotiating the ditches and potholes between the house and the street. I'm out last.

We ride the 7 kilometers to the main highway in a parade fashion, everyone riding faster than we would be able to maintain. Bike bells do their dinging. We wave greetings to everyone outside their homes doing their morning chores. Men look up from their gardening and women from their laundry to wave and give big smiles. Children run along with us. One young boy on a bicycle rides as hard as he can to keep up, even racing ahead for a while, until he runs out of steam.

When we arrive at the main road, final good-byes are said. Mumba offers a prayer for our safety and sends us on our way. I note that he's not going with us.

This main highway connecting Lubumbashi with the mining towns to the west is hard-packed gravel, macadam, wide and dusty. The trucks that run on it are big and fast. Although a lot of bicycles travel this road, it is dangerous. It is also teeth-rattling rough. For those two reasons, a single-track foot/bike path had been created by those walking/riding along the road. It is uneven and unpredictable, sometimes disappearing entirely and forcing us back onto the road, but it is smoother and safer than the road. We are off on an adventure, the size of which none of us had yet experienced. It is now too late to ask, "Do you really think we can do this?" I'm thinking to myself, *I have no idea what we're doing, and neither do they. There is no plan, no safety net, no clue.*

Prospère and I feel the need for speed and take the lead. Prospère greets everyone we pass with a laugh and a wave. This is fun for him, and I resonate with his joy.

Éléphant and Shabana lag behind. Éléphant is a strong man, but he is not bicycle strong, and he will ride a bicycle only as far as Mulungwishi. There he'll give his bicycle to Mulongo and pick up his motorcycle, which is in Mulungwishi for repair, and prep for this trip. He's going to make today's ride, but this is clearly not his thing. Shabana's lack of strength concerns me. He is not keeping up, and I fear he is not going to be able to finish. He is fighting back from a bout of typhoid fever last year.

Mulongo has gone ahead by bus to make arrangements for our overnight stay and to check on the motorcycle. We are inventing this as we go.

Prospère and I set the pace fast. The faster we go, the more the shock waves pound through our wrists, up our arms, and into our whole bodies. As often as we can, we opt for the footpaths running beside the road. They are rambling, rolling, and narrow, and they require constant attention, but they are smooth on the wheels. We jump back and forth from one side of the highway to the other, avoiding pedestrians and ditches.

Even in the rainy season, this country is dusty and dry. It will rain, but the sun will dry everything instantly, and the trucks kick up the red dust. This is not the jungle scene of Africa. There is no wild game. It's open industrial country with strip mines frequently visible from the road. It's a big road with big trucks and big power lines, yet small groups of people also move along the road with no connection to the road's industrial purpose. Wrecks on this road are common and often fatal. Bicycles are given no respect and are like bugs to these big trucks. There are two worlds here: the world of the mining companies, and the world of the people who live on the land. Disconnected.

The sun slowly burns off the morning mist, dries everything, and begins to slowly warm the day. There is no shade. By midday, it is hot. Dusty, thirsty, and suffering, we ride through the heat. There are no shortcuts.

With our bicycles fully loaded and heavy, the road gives us a good pace of 14–15 kilometers per hour, sometimes hitting in the 30s on smooth sections and even the high 30s on downhills. At the bottom of most hills, there is a bridge broken up by deadly potholes, so we can't take downhills too fast.

It's frustrating that the road is so rough that we can't make better time. I want to have one fast day on a fast road because I know that once we leave this road, it will be slow going. This is forcing me to learn a new pace of life. This trip is not going to be a sprint. I have to settle in for the long haul.

We are going to make the 80 kilometers to Mulungwishi in good time despite the disappointing pace. Some sections between villages are long. Some of the hills are a challenge, and the dust raised by the trucks clings to the sweat on our bodies. Nonetheless, despite the heat in this barren, unattractive country, this is a good day on the road.

For years I've avoided even taking a camera along. Ten years ago, you could go straight to jail for pulling out a camera. Railroads, bridges, roads, and buildings were all considered military targets and off-limits to photography. Then there was the sensitivity of the people. There is a general shame in the state of the country and for many a personal shame in their own poverty, and the camera-toting tourist is an ugly thing. I had determined to do a better job of documenting this trip with more photos. Among friends the camera is welcome. Everyone wants to pose for an individual or family portrait. But candid shots, not so much. Catching people in their daily lives is difficult.

We're coasting fast down a hill on the hard gravel, avoiding potholes around the corner in the bridge. We come across a truck that has overturned off a bridge and is hanging upside down in an awkward pose. Looks like a great photo op. I look around and don't see anyone, so I sneak the camera out for a snap of the overturned truck—and hate myself and this feeling of voyeurism.

As soon as I snap the photo, a man comes running up the road yelling at me. Where did he come from?

I'm upset, not fearful of what he might do to me, but that I was caught doing something I hate in others. I was caught being an ugly tourist. Despite my commitment to take photos that show the good in the people of the Congo, I was caught taking a lousy photo that is an embarrassment to them.

Éléphant gets to the man before he gets to me, and the shouting becomes two-way. Then it runs its course and slows. Éléphant explains that we are a team of United Methodists, which turns the conflict. This man is United Methodist, and we are now on the same team, of the same tribe.

As members of the same tribe, we get the real story. The truck had overturned a couple months ago. The village is required to remove it but doesn't have the money to hire another truck to pull it out. The photo would not only shame them, but it could also get them into to real trouble with the government. I offer to delete the picture, but everyone now thinks there is no problem.

Here is a dilemma we're discovering: Midlevel community leaders are in the no-win position of having responsibility and no funding. I didn't yet realize it, but this grappling with unfunded mandates would become an entry point of our work.

I put the camera back deep in my pannier and won't pull it out again until Kyubo.

The deep regret in my soul is that I've seen so much that I can't show you. A lot, because I didn't take a camera or had to keep the camera in my bag. A lot, also, because when I did take a picture, it just didn't reflect what I saw. You have to be here to experience both the beauty and the brokenness.

Back on the road, we move on from the overturned truck, and around two in the afternoon, we pass through a small village with shops and shade. We stop, have a couple of biscuits (cookies) and sodas. I have a Coke, but the rest of the team prefers Fanta. Often, there isn't a choice, or maybe there's a choice between Coke and Fanta, but no diet anything, which is OK with me. Increasingly, different flavors of Fanta and sometimes Sprite are available, but this is not the land of choices. Glass bottles are giving way to cans and plastic bottles. Bottled water, Dasani, is available, especially along the trucking routes.

# *Mulungwishi*

Our break is followed by a long afternoon of riding. I'm not totally spent by the time we arrive at Mulungwishi and perk up when I begin to see familiar landmarks. I spot the cross made of 55-gallon oil drums on the top of the mountain overlooking the seminary. Then we cross the railroad track where the road makes a sharp S curve before going vertical. Open country turns into village life, with trees and homes and children and goats and chickens, and clothes on the lines and cooking fires.

Mulungwishi is an old Methodist mission station. In fact, the first Methodist missionaries to the Congo are buried here. It has its financial struggles, but there is no hint that it is going away. It is presently in a legal battle to save its mountain from invading Chinese mining companies. The seminary trains clergy and others for service in both the southern Congo and the North Katanga episcopal areas and has faculty members from both. American missionaries David and Lori Persons live and work here, and Jeff Hoover comes from Lubumbashi to teach. The Persons are both second-generation missionaries here. However, the mission has made the transition from missionary-run to indigenous leadership.

It is a hard, long push up a steep hill from the village to the seminary, not something you welcome at the end of a full day's ride. There is still plenty of life in the legs, and Prospère and I race up the hill. Éléphant and Shabana are still several kilometers behind us. The team is housed halfway up the road to the big house in one of the original missionary houses now converted to a guesthouse. It looks like colonial Africa, European architecture artificially placed in the jungle, but now, years later, tired and run down, bearing the marks of the changes it has weathered.

Leaving my Congolese team members behind, I am taken to the big house. This is the old missionary pattern, which will have changed by the next time we visit Mulungwishi, not because I will change it, but because the relationship between the faculty at Mulungwishi and Friendly Planet Missiology will grow. But this year, no one knows what we are doing, including the team and me. We're using old models until we can discover a new one.

The last time I was in this house back in 1998, a Danish missionary was living here, a young single architect named Klaus. He was in constant conflict with Bishop Katembo of the Southern Congo Conference, who had him building a massive church in Kolwezi. The bishop's dreams were Klaus' engineering nightmares, the mostly normal arguments between a client and an architect. But the big fights were over the money. Klaus publicly accused the bishop of misappropriation of funds earmarked for construction. Whoa—major breach in protocol. But that was also a time of transition for the relationships between white missionaries and the Congolese bishops. Klaus was in that first generation of missionaries with special skills and invited by the Congolese bishops to fill specific talent gaps.

Klaus was the next-generation techie for the missionary community. He had a satellite setup for e-mail, which seemed like spy stuff in the late 1990s. In fact, he had encryption software because missionaries worried that the government monitored their e-mail traffic and any innocent comment might be taken as politically subversive. Klaus' system was the only way that e-mail could reach my wife, Teri, back home in Indiana, so I would get on my bike and ride two hours from Likasi to Mulungwishi to send an e-mail home. E-mails from Teri would come to me hand delivered by anyone who happened to be traveling through Mulungwishi on the way to Likasi. One rainy day, I was sitting on a stoop on the Likasi campus, just out of the rain, as a runner approached with a folded piece of paper: an e-mail from home. It could have been David Livingstone receiving mail by runner. This is Africa.

Then again, maybe Klaus was a spy. Of course, he wasn't—missionary would be a dumb cover for a spy—but the Congolese believed that certain, if not all, American missionaries worked for the CIA. It's hard to overstate the paranoia of those days.

To add to my own personal doubt, when we were evacuated from the DRC in late 1998, a suit from the U.S. Embassy showed up in Kitwe (Zambia) to debrief us. The stated concern was for identifying any remaining Americans in the DRC, but nevertheless, we were passing along intelligence to the U.S. government. Our Congolese colleagues were correct in assuming that when the shooting started, we missionaries would show our true loyalties and be safely secreted away. (This suit—in fact a consul from the embassy—had the very same position now held by my son-in-law.)

The model for the relationship between missionary and indigenous church leader has not yet changed much. In 2010 my team and I eat separate meals. I share the guesthouse with Jeff Hoover. I'm sure he is thoroughly confused by my expedition. I'm worried that he's laughing inside at my ignorance and naivety. It's entirely possible, though, that he doesn't care at all. He has his head buried in his laptop, busy with his own teaching preparations. Jeff, with his Yale PhD, is serious about the quality of education here. All the faculty members take their work seriously. They consider this to be a first-rate seminary, and all evidence is that it is.

After we've bathed and eaten, the team meets with the Congolese leadership of the seminary. The question on everyone's mind is "Why?" Why ride a bicycle?" The group around the table, our team and the seminary faculty, eventually craft an answer. The "why" is to identify with the suffering of the people. This is really swimming against the social current and even a bit threatening to the faculty. These are leaders who have risen through the ranks and arrived at a point of considerable status. The idea of choosing to suffer with the people is strange. They've been there, done that. The goal of life is to move up the social and economic ladders, not down. Besides that, they aren't out of the woods yet themselves. Mulungwishi is underfunded, and the faculty members suffer to put food on their own tables. They take a run at recruiting our efforts for their cause, but we are on our way north to the remote districts. Instead, we tell them that a United Methodist student bicycling group at Purdue University has raised money for bicycles for the seminary. This is received as good news, and thanks are given.

## *Mulungwishi to New Mind*

*I*n the morning Mulongo, our team leader, takes charge. He likes to get out at first light. Éléphant has his motorcycle. We take a team photo in front of the seminary sign. We're off. The ride from Tenke to Mulungwishi was 80 kilometers yesterday. Mulongo wants to cover 100 today.

It's another cool, damp morning just like yesterday. It rained through the night, and the road is wet. The mist is so thick that it's like riding through a wall of cool water. As in the morning before, I'm in a T-shirt, but the other riders are wearing their jackets. I marvel at seeing winter coats here. I guess it's like a 55 degree day in Wisconsin feeling balmy and a 55 degree day in Florida feeling cool. I have no idea what the temperature is.

After about an hour, the sun has cooked off the fog and the road turns to steam. By the second hour, everything is dry, and the heat begins to build.

We have a good morning's ride to Lwambo, a busy town with electricity, a cell tower, and shops along a street filled with trucks and motorcycles.

We stop in front of a shop, and the shopkeeper sets out chairs for us on his small front patio. As everywhere, the blue plastic lawn chairs that would be low end in America are first class here. Mulongo finds us a six-pack of cold Cokes. I am a traveling Coca-Cola commercial. Take a photo outside a bodega in Lwambo, put music to it, and you have the stuff Coke commercials are made of.

I pull out my netbook and Vodacom modem to try to connect to the Internet to make a Facebook status update and, if possible, send a personal message to Teri. No joy. The cell tower in town is Zain, not Vodacom. There's a Vodacom tower a few kilometers north of Lwambo. I'll try there.

This is the team's last opportunity to buy things to take up-country to family and friends, and we disperse into the shops. Éléphant has taken the fourth bicycle and modified it into a third-wheel cart for his motorcycle, and we load this brilliant piece of engineering with 2-liter Dasani (a Coke product) water bottles. I fill all four of my water bottles with bottled water.

The team regroups and we're off again. Not too far out of town, we stop at the Vodacom cell tower. I send out a message that I learn later will be my last until we arrive at Mulongo. I have to ask the team to stop, and I feel as though the group doesn't understand my need to communicate with home. This is disappointing evidence that we're not yet on the same page.

From Lwambo we leave the east-west mine road and head north, going vertical on the map. We're leaving behind the towns along the road where the shops have all we need. Here is where the adventure really begins. The condition of the road north is not too bad so far. It's mostly hard-packed sand. There are occasional puddles of water, but nothing that slows us, and we're clipping along at a good pace.

Mulongo pulls along beside me and in high spirits announces, "This is my first adventure."

I respond, "Man, you live in Africa."

We both laugh. I know that Mulongo has ridden this road many times. It isn't the first time that he has done what we are about to do. It is, however, the first time he has done it with this sense of adventure.

Then the state of the road in the rainy season hits us. There is water crossing the road, water that is several yards wide and too deep to ride through. It even has a current. The road has become a river.

We have to carry everything through the water, and this is where I come face to face with my physical limitations. In spite of the fact that I'm determined to carry my own weight, the truth is that I'm not physically strong enough to carry the weight of my loaded bicycle across this water, and Éléphant insists that he carry my bike across. I remind myself that my bike's pannier system is carrying equipment that is here for the good of the whole team: the water filter, first aid kit, tent, and many of the gifts we've received.

Éléphant is not big, but he is super strong. He lifts my bike over his head and carries it through the knee-deep water. This is an exchange of dignity more than an act of servitude. As a senior member of the community, Éléphant is more my age than the others. He has worked for missionaries in the past and is old school in understanding his role on the team—to make sure I get to Mulongo safely. In all matters mechanical and safety, Éléphant is in charge.

Éléphant is also prepared and has rubber fishing boots to wear for this first water crossing of the expedition. The rest of us remove our shoes, put on our flip-flops, roll up our pants, and cross the water.

By the middle of the afternoon, we are back on our bikes approaching Bunkeya. The last kilometer is a steep climb, and everyone else pushes his bike up the hill. I try to keep pedaling and almost make it to the top. The advantage I have is in the Cannondale T1's gearing.

At the top of the hill, an old brick sign with a painted lion welcomes us to Bunkeya, which feels more like a town than a village. We have to descend to get to the town spread out over the valley before us. A Congolese village is a beautiful sight from above: neat rows of grass-roofed houses under groves of banana trees. All I'm thinking is that I hope that we don't have to climb back out to leave town. The hill down into town is steep, and we ride fast, hating to waste brake, flying past administrative buildings and schools, then stores.

We have a problem in Bunkeya. The Southern Congo episcopal area's Bishop Katembo is a friend, but the district superintendent here has no motivation to provide extraordinary hospitality, and this is the first stop along the way where we really do need the local hospitality. Mulongo is frustrated that we are not met as we enter town, and someone has to be sent to find the district superintendent, who is still in his field. Although Mulongo is embarrassed that arrangements have fallen through on this, our first stop up-country, it's not too big a deal, unless this is the way it's going to be the whole trip. The added pressure is that Mulongo insists on covering 100 kilometers today, and we're losing precious time in Bunkeya.

A *bukari* meal for the team is wrestled together. The accepted belief is that *wazungu* don't/can't/won't eat Congolese food, so I get bread and a fried egg. We each get a Fanta. Mulongo is eager to get us back on the road and ride 20 more kilometers before dark.

Back on the road we're still trying to find our pace. On good roads and while I'm still fresh, I'm faster than the others. Prospère is strong out of the gate and enjoys riding fast with me. My preferred pace is fast with a shade break every 10 kilometers or so, which is about how far villages are apart. Mulongo, on the other hand, is slow and steady. He can ride forever at his pace. He never wants to break. There he is in his orange surfer T-shirt—steady, never tired.

I recognize the orange surfboard-themed T-shirt as one that our son, Robbie, had given to Mulongo. There is a strange otherworldly experience seeing a familiar object so far from home.

At 6:00 the sun goes down, but the dark comes slowly, and we'll have good light for another hour or so. It's raining steadily, but not too hard. I'm counting the kilometers in French. I love the mental gymnastics of counting in the nineties: four score and thirteen, four score and fourteen. At 100 kilometers, I wonder where we are going to stop. We're not near anything. Usually, when approaching a town or even a village, we see some signs of civilization 2 or 3 kilometers out, but 100 kilometers from Mulungwishi, we're still deep in the bush.

Then Mulongo pulls into a tiny village that I don't see until we pull over, maybe five huts hidden in the small trees.

We exchange greeting with the villagers, who are friendly and even invite us to take their pictures. I ask the team for the name of the village: New Mind. To this day I don't know if stopping in New Mind was Mulongo's plan all along, or if he picked the first place after 100 kilometers to stop.

The rain has stopped, and we negotiate for a space to put up our tents—the one I brought from Indiana and the one Mulongo bought from an Irish NGO—for the first time. Shabana shares with me, while Prospère bunks with Mulongo. Éléphant chooses to sleep outside. In the morning we take enough time to shake the night's rain and the morning dew from our equipment as we pack.

# *Daydreaming*

$\mathcal{E}$ ighty to 100 kilometers a day means a lot of hours on the bike. Because I now don't have to give all my attention to large trucks and dangerous pot-holes, I daydream. On the bike I write my sermons, plan for the future, and spin my story to justify my existence. Mostly the wanderings in my mind fall into three categories: French numbers, Fort Myers Beach, and this book.

I watch the numbers go by on the cycle computer keeping track of our journey. I get a panicked feeling any time it is not working, which is contrary to my commitment to release all need to be in control or to know what is coming up. Last year, I went into the Geographical Institute in Lubumbashi and asked for a map. They pulled out an old master, dated 1961, and burned me a copy on a blueprint machine. As we set out, these navigation tools are important only to me and I'm not the navigator. The group has no need of my map or my bicycle computer.

They all know that I have these tools, but I refrain from announcing our distance covered or pulling out the map just to satisfy my curiosity. This is going to be a dis-cipline of the trip: To go deeper into listening, I must first curb my personal curios-ity and my need to know. I'm aware that this is counterlogical, but my questions are not the right questions yet.

A few kilometers out on the road, I realize that the computer isn't working, and feelings of panic mixed with shame mixed with frustration mixed with perfection-ism set upon me. I check the relationship of the pickup sensor on the front fork and the little magnetic marker fastened to a spoke of the wheel. When they are lined up properly, the sensor counts the times the marker goes by. They check out. Still no joy.

I'm regretting having bought the wireless model. The problem with expensive bike parts is that once you're on the road in the Congo, they either work or don't work. There's no shop around to fix or replace them. We've barely started our journey, and this tool has failed.

Then it hits me: This is wireless. It works with a radio signal. The wireless signal is being disrupted by the magnetic field of the watch I had put on the handlebar next to the computer to see the time, to relieve the discomfort of sweat under the watch-band on my wrist, and, of course, to prevent a white band forming around my wrist as my arm cooked tan in the hot sun. I take the watch off the handlebar and place it in the pocket of one of the back panniers. *Ça marche.*

Putting the watch in the pannier solves the computer malfunction but creates a new problem: The watch is solar powered, and the pocket is dark. Takes me just a day to figure that one out.

I curse myself for panicking over something that I can live without. The team doesn't need the cycle computer. It is a big deal only to me. It shouldn't be a big deal. I don't have to know. On the other hand, counting the kilometers is a mental exercise that passes the time as the ride hits long stretches of monotony.

Here's the thing: French numbers are funny, especially when you get into the six-ties to nineties. Sixty-one is normal, but seventy-one is said as "sixty eleven." Eighty is "four twenty," and ninety is "four twenty ten." Ninety-nine is "four twenty ten nine." Eventually, though, I do learn that Congolese French speakers use the Bel-gian system, in which seventy is seventy and ninety is ninety.

I'm riding along in the hot sun counting the kilometers in French and talking to myself like a crazy person. This is crazy and I'm going crazy in the sun. "Only mad dogs and Englishmen go out in the midday sun."

It is hot, and I'm being roasted in the burning sun.

The second category of my daydreaming is Fort Myers Beach, Florida. My wife, Teri, is a schoolteacher, and her spring break is a fixed point in our calendar. Every-thing else can float. I can be late or early to any other appointment, I can wander without purpose through Africa, but I must be back for spring break.

We'll spend the break with friends at a mom-and-pop motel in Fort Myers Beach. It's not fancy at all, but it is right on the beach, and that's all that we care about.

The rest of my mental time is spent imagining what I'd write in a book. I talk to myself about the journey itself, the condition of the road, the colors of the grass and sky, the birds, the songs of my companions, the rock formations that come straight out of *The Lion King,* and the things that look as normal to me as an Indiana cornfield. I talk to myself about the mechanical systems of my bicy-cle, about the team's bicycles, about farmers and fishermen we meet along the road, about chickens and goats and laughing children. There are women cook-ing, children running, young men posing, old men playing checkers, and chick-ens and goats crossing the road. Broken-down cars and trucks are monuments in village yards. The strangest cars are in the strangest places. How did they get that here? I want to tell you about everything I see, but I don't have the picture words to describe this world. Every detail is fascinating to me, but maybe you wouldn't even be interested. This is a story that must be lived, not told, but I want you to know it, so I will tell you this story in writing and hope that its greatness overcomes my limitations.

# Kyubo, Mitwaba District

*W*e're riding through an area known as *Le Triangle de la Mort,* the Triangle of Death, on *La Route Rouge,* the Red Road, so named because of the blood of the killings in all of the villages along this road. It just so happens that the sand of the road is also red. I'm reminded of the country road that led to my grandfather's house when I was a kid. That road was also red, from the red shale of the coal mines.

The destination for today is Kyubo, 75 kilometers from New Mind. The riding is not bad: water on the road, but not too much; a bit of rain, but that kept the sun from beating down on us. We stop for our only break for the day at Gar Karila, a major crossroads where the Red Road meets an east-west ridge trail. You can turn left and arrive in Lubudi eventually. There is local food for sale, some roasted *bukari* in leaves, but no packaged food or bottled water.

By kilometer 70, I'm dragging after a full day of hill riding. In the early afternoon, the sun has come out, and it's hot. We hit bad mud that eats my skinny tires, and I can no longer ride. Then the others give in to the mud. We all have to get off and push.

Just as we're getting off to push, Boy Scouts show up. They've come from Kyubo to greet us and to take our bikes. This is great!

Kyubo is at the southern edge of the Mitwaba District, the largest and most isolated district of North Katanga. An appointment to the Mitwaba District is like being sent to Siberia. We came into Kyubo with a returning hero's welcome. At the district line, we are met by the district superintendent, the United Methodist Women, several pastors, and a youth choir. Scouts are pushing our bicycles, we're tromping in the mud, heads and whole bodies are slumping from the heat and exhaustion, but other than that, we're feeling pretty good now that the ride is over for the day. The district lay leader offers us a 2-liter bottle of Dasani. God bless the Coca-Cola Bottling Company and its global reach! I open it, but my U.S. Marine Corps training prevents me from drinking until all in the team drink; meanwhile my thirst makes me anxious about there being enough for all of us, meaning me.

Three young girls in white blouse school uniforms present us with flowers, and the pastor's daughter recites a welcome speech in English.

After hugs and handshakes all around, we walk ceremoniously over to a parcel of land with a sign in front that says that this concession (a gift from the land chief) is for The United Methodist Church, Kyubo Parish. There is nothing there except the overgrown rubble of the footprint of a church burned to the ground five years earlier and three black wooden crosses, which, we're told, mark the mass graves of those killed when the village was overrun three times during the war. We stop for prayer.

I now know why we're making this trip: We are making pastoral calls on villages that were destroyed in the war and have been forgotten by the rest of the world. I had no idea when we set out that this is what we would find. The people of this village, and villages just like it all along the Red Road, feel totally abandoned by the world. This is the first visit by anyone representing the church from the outside world since the war.

Leaving the war-damaged church site, we sing and parade through the village to the current church building and parsonage. The parsonage is typical of the homes our pastors live in, four small rooms in a weather-beaten square house. Women sitting outside along the front of the house are washing and cutting vegetables, preparing a meal for us, and children are hanging on to the women. The church is a temporary construction with low walls of unfired mud bricks and a grass roof. It is a place to worship until a new church can be built on the concession.

Ducking our heads to get through the doorway, we follow our hosts into the church and up to the chancel area where plastic chairs have been set for us. The congregation joins us around the altar, which is draped with a baby blanket and adorned with plastic flowers in a Sprite can, and we have church. The district superintendent gives the welcome speech and we respond with our thanks for the hospitality.

After this church service, some Cokes and Fantas appear, and we sit and wait for the meal. This is significant. These drinks are expensive, and the farther north we get, the harder it is to find them. I suspect that Mulongo is subsidizing them with our funds. Meanwhile, Éléphant is busy with getting all our bicycles, his motorcycle, and equipment into the church. He's strung up a mosquito net where he will sleep tonight. I'm offered a bath: a bucket of water, a bar of soap, and a towel in a small grass outhouse dedicated to bathing.

Finally, we're called to the table that is set for us in the front room of the parsonage. It's a full Congolese spread, featuring large quantities of *bukari,* chicken, goat, palm sauce, greens, and rice for the *mzungu*. Éléphant is a rice eater also, the only Congolese I know who doesn't eat *bukari,* and he gets kidded about that a lot.

We haven't had an Internet connection since that cell tower just north of Lwambo. There is no cell tower here, but they say that there is a Belgian in the village with Internet and he is willing to let us use it. This is too curious not to pursue. Another white person in the village is rare. There's a new resort being built in Kyubo below the waterfall. We parade down to the construction site, passing roaring rapids on our left and a grass airstrip on our right. We arrive at a large guarded gate and gatehouse. Phone calls are made, and eventually we are let into a world that seems totally out of place. Here's an African safari resort going up in the shadow of a village destroyed by war.

The Belgian turns out to be a South African, and not a friendly one. He has not agreed to our using his Internet after all, even though he is working online when we arrive. For the construction phase of the resort, his office and home are a series of large tents and tarps, which create a space that is like being outdoors but under canvas.

We are offered, however, a tour of the unfinished resort. It is indeed an impressive place, designed to provide a real African experience for the rich and famous. These future guests will fly in by helicopter from Lubumbashi because no one who has the money to stay here is going to come up by road, and certainly not by bicycle.

The resort sits at the base of a wide waterfall with maybe a 100-foot drop. On one side, the developers have built a hydroelectric plant that will provide electricity for the resort and the whole village. There is so much water power in the Congo that every home should have free electricity.

I am selfishly hoping that there is an offer of a bed in one of the not yet finished bungalows, but we walk back to the village where I'm given a bed in the pastor's house, the best they have.

# Macarthur Has Returned!

Our entrance into Kyubo is the Congolese equivalent of a ticker-tape parade. The villagers are welcoming me back as their missionary, despite the fact that my status as their missionary twelve years ago was more projection than reality.

In 1997, the General Board of Global Ministries of The United Methodist Church (GBGM) offered me an eighteen-month contract because Bishop Ntambo had requested me. My contract assigned me to be the incoming director of the Likasi School of Theology, replacing a PhD couple who had left six months before. Although that was what the GBGM needed, that was not why I had accepted the commission, and I worked quickly to get myself free of that job. Bishop Ntambo called me up to Kamina to commission me a missionary in the North Katanga Conference, and this was the real commissioning for me. Even though the GBGM was paying me, in my heart and soul, I was working for Bishop Ntambo.

At the commissioning in Kamina, the bishop gave me two assignments: the Lubudi District and the Mitwaba District. How could I direct a seminary and be the resident missionary in two noncontiguous districts? The assignments came without instructions, but I was to learn that communities here are used to having nonresident chiefs and patrons, and I was now, like it or not, the appointed patron of the Lubudi and Mitwaba Districts.

It was during my first visit to the Mitwaba District in 1998 that the GBGM ordered all United Methodist missionaries to evacuate because of the war in eastern Congo.

The seminary at Likasi didn't survive the war. The fiscal structure of the seminary depended on support from outside, and the only way to get that support was to have a missionary. Once I left, there was no one found to follow me. The money dried up and the school closed. Eventually, Bishop Ntambo opened Kamina Methodist University, where it is possible to run a school on the local economy, and that university now includes a faculty for theology.

I had been in the Mitwaba District only a matter of days before the evacuation, and now after a twelve-year absence, the villagers are welcoming me back home as their missionary.

# Kyubo to Kasengeshi

In the morning the district superintendent of the Mitwaba District and another pastor ride out of town with us, which matches my old plan of picking up a rider or two for a day or two, then a fresh set in the next district.

In the cool moist air of sunrise, we cross the bridge over the river above the falls. It seems my companions take no notice of the view, but I have to stop to take it in. Pink streaks in a blue sky meet the mist rising from the falls. I think it is the perfect start of a perfect day of riding. I get back on my bike and quickly catch up with the team.

We are rolling at a brisk pace. We would be in Kasengeshi in no time at all. But no—just 5 kilometers into the ride, we stop at a small rural church. I am annoyed that we are stopping when we had just gotten going and I'm concerned that if we stop at every church 5 kilometers apart, this is going to be a long day. However, this turns out to be a good stop. I fall in love with this church. It is newly built from locally fired bricks by the congregation members themselves. The artistry of their grass roof can be seen from the inside looking up. It's all fresh and smells of new grass. The people gather for singing and a short worship with us. Unfortunately I know that without a metal roof, a church like this has a life expectancy of three years. The weather will take down all the love and skill that went into the construction of this church.

We're back on the road for the long day's ride. No more stops. Heads down for Kasengeshi.

# The Process

As we ride, my brain is busy putting together a seminar on missiology for young pastors. I can't help but believe that we could teach a new model, and I know the model: Dr. David Hilton's Process based on Paulo Freire's work on generative themes.

David Hilton taught me everything I know about a completely new way to do mission work. He called it the *Process*. Actually, he didn't teach me anything I didn't already know, and that is the genius of the Process.

Dr. Hilton was a United Methodist medical missionary in West Africa in the 1980s. For ten years he did what he referred to as the "jungle heroics" of six to eight surgeries a day. At the end of his tenth year, he woke up and realized that the health of the community he had come to serve was no better than it was the day he had arrived. He walked out of the jungle to find a better way. Hilton became an early advocate of creating health up-front, rather than treating disease after, and as the doctor for all the missionaries employed by the General Board of Global Ministries of The United Methodist Church (GBGM), he preached the gospel of living toward health rather than the Western model of disease treatment. Wellness was a radical model back then.

Around that time, Hilton also found the work of Paulo Freire.

Freire worked in Brazil's Ministry of Education in the 1970s. He was charged with finding a solution for the alarmingly low rate in adult literacy. After years of failing to find a program that would teach adults how to read, Freire gave up. Like Hilton, he went looking for a different model. Freire sat in public places where regular working class people gathered: barbershops, laundromats, markets. He listened. He listened for months. He began writing down what he came to call *generative themes:* subjects that raise the emotional level in the room. Some generative themes make everyone angry, like the working class getting screwed again by the government. Some generative themes make everyone thrilled, like Brazil going to the World Cup. Often, however, generative themes split the community, like a multinational corporation bringing in a new factory; for some, that means economic growth and jobs, while for others, it means the loss of hard-won union contracts.

When Freire created reading materials around these generative themes, adults learned quickly to read. Poor adults began to read and then became politically active around the issues that they were reading about, not because someone told they should be, but because the reading material reflected back to them their own generative themes. This political activity led to a peasant land revolt, forcing land reform in the country. Freire laid out this model of generative themes in his *Pedagogy of the Oppressed.*

Hilton taught his workshop on the Process in the pedagogical model of Paulo Freire. We were on the third day of the training when I realized that we were immersed in the Process. I had fully expected to attend classes where the instructor would write all the steps of the Process on the board, and then I would write them in my notebook and apply them when I got to the field. Sitting in this workshop, however—if you could even call it a workshop—was like sitting with Yoda. Hilton said almost nothing and seemed to have no agenda of his own, but the peace around him drew out from each of the members of the group all the wisdom we hadn't yet learned to trust.

Hilton's process is built on Freire's pedagogy, which is related to the Latin American liberation theology movement of the mid-twentieth century. In our day, this has become the school of practical theology. Theologians like to joke that practical theology is opposed to "the other kind of theology," but it's a misleading joke. Practical theology focuses on the *praxis,* the practice of the church or community, and reflects theologically on the actions. This is a reversal of the order of reflection as related to action in classical theology, which moves from *doxis* (what we say we believe) to our actions.

*Scripture as a Tool of Community Development,* my Doctor of Ministry thesis in practical theology, argues that the difference between practical theology and classical theology is a big deal in the way we carry out mission, although we are often unaware or unwilling to be aware. In one way, we already know the answers, and we enter a community with answers in hand. The other way, we enter a community with eyes wide open in order to see what we were not able to see when we were blinded by our own beliefs, both theological and cultural. What is even a bigger deal is that with the second way, we have to be seriously prepared to reflect theologically on the activities of the community and any church or agency that has come to help. This is the unique contribution of the church. No one else can do this. No one else is equipped to do this. No one else is called to do this. The one thing lacking in all our development work, however, is theological reflection. I'm out here in the field, and trust me, there is *no* theological reflection being done. At the very best, there might be some evaluation of a set of projects, although it seems that the money runs out long before any evaluation can happen. And for you United Methodists out there, the most underappreciated and underutilized theology in the field is John Wesley's. I would argue that Wesley was an early adopter of practical theology.

A quick and dirty minitutorial on the Process as we ride along:

Step one, listen. You listen, then you listen some more. When you think you know something, stop yourself from speaking and listen some more. Listen until what you thought you knew is no longer what you know. Listen until you know nothing at all. Let everything you thought you knew fade into nothingness. Listen with your whole body and soul. Sit and listen. Ride and listen. Don't talk. Listen.

Listen.

Listen.

Listen.

Step one will take months, years. Seriously. This can't be done in a day and it can't be done in a survey. In my opinion all community research tools are rubbish. People are going to tell you what they think you want to hear. Or, more importantly, they don't know yet what they know, because what they know is buried in layers of what they have been told they should know. You have to listen long enough to get below the level of what everybody believes that they should know to what they really do know. Listen. And when you have listened until there can't possibly be anything else out there to hear, listen some more.

I want to listen beyond what other missionaries have told me about the Congolese people. Those bits of friendly advice must disappear. But also, I want to listen beyond what the Congolese people tell me about themselves. There is something deep in their knowledge that they don't know that they know. There will be truths to discover, but those truths won't be on the surface.

Let me be clear here. This deep listening is appropriate anywhere with any group. It is, however, common in a patronage system that all parties have bought into a story that explains their problems that only serves to reinforce those problems. The listener has to get on the other side of this story.

What are you listening for? You're listening for what Freire called generative themes. These are not the things that you see need to be fixed in the community. These are not the things that you just know are killing the babies. These are not the projects that you're sure must be started right now. These are the themes that, when brought up, excite the community. Everybody has something to say about them.

A caution here: Be aware that the members of the community may give you what the last visiting development agency told them that they need to work on. Beware of parroting.

Step two: Reflect the generative theme back to the community in what Freire called a *code*. A code can be a cartoon or a drama or a song that presents the theme in a slightly different telling, matching the theme, but telling it in a fresh way. It is critical to understanding the Process that a code does *not* present an answer. The purpose of the code is to force the responsibility for the creation of a solution back on the community.

The scriptures of all traditions are rich in codes. Jesus' parables are examples of effective Freirian codes drawn from the Bible. It is important, however, that the preacher does not use Scripture to push an answer. This is probably the hardest thing for preachers to get or accept. In this model, you are not using Scripture to tell people what to do, but to see what is happening in their lives. Save the answers for later. First, we must discover the questions.

Here's the good news: When you spend the time up-front in listening and discipline yourself to holding the answers, once the question is determined, you find that the community has had the answer all along. The people just didn't know they had the answer. This is key. If you are the giver of answers, then when you leave—and you will leave—you take the answers with you. When the community members discover that they know the answers, those answers never leave.

Oh, another thought: What happens if you misread the generative theme? What if you get it wrong? No problem. It's not about you, and it doesn't require your brilliance. Just follow the Process. When you hit a generative theme, the room comes alive. If you feed back a code that doesn't hit a real generative theme, it will fall flat, and you need to move on. Go back around again and try something else.

## On the Way to Kasengeshi


*M*idday we climb a hill to the village of Mukana. The women of the church have planned a full meal for us. There's a grass-roofed pavilion that serves as a local market. Plastic lawn chairs are brought out, and the team and I rest in the shade while the meal is prepared. We are slowed down by hospitality, but this long break is welcome. It's been a hot ride in full sun.

But our rest is short lived. The director of the local school has arrived and wants to show us his school. We're up out of our comfortable chairs in the shade and into the hot sun to walk to see this school. My patience is challenged. I'm learning how to not be in charge of my life, including when I get to rest. One of the comical dynamics of the patronage system is that the patron works for the clients.

What we find is a typical schoolyard, half a dozen individual classroom-sized brick buildings arranged in a square pattern around a football pitch. What is not typical is that one of these classrooms is not like the rest. It is built of fired bricks with a cement floor and a metal roof. Inside are new steel desks for the students. The other classrooms are sad with failing walls, dirt floors, weathered grass roofs, and bricks for seats. UNICEF had come right after the war with a wave of help. It is now gone and the director wants to know when it will return to finish the school.

UNICEF is not returning. The world has moved on to other crises.

I'm supposing that UNICEF intended for this one classroom to be a model for the others, that the community would finish the school. What I think it has done is to deliver just enough help to teach the community that the solution to the community's problems is coming from an outside NGO. All of their attention is turned toward recruiting an NGO like UNICEF, or a missionary like me, to build their school.

In fairness to the director, he is not lazy. He is not sitting and waiting for UNICEF to return, or a missionary to visit. He works hard, but it takes all his time and effort just to keep the grass roofs repaired. He has no time for curriculum development.

I'm puzzling on what I've been shown as we walk back to lunch, and thinking again about how I might use the Process to get the community to own this problem and use its own wisdom and local assets to build the school, rather than wait for someone from outside to arrive. I'm thinking again about generative themes and codes.

The lunch is a feast. There are generous portions of all the traditional dishes. I'm amazed at the level of hospitality, knowing that the cost of this hospitality far exceeds any possible return on investment. While appreciating the generosity and the good food, I can't help but be troubled by a system where a poor community spends all its resources on entertaining a prospective patron, expecting the patron to then deliver the help they need. I doubt this is conscious. I don't think that the hospitality is not genuine. I don't think that they have conspired to trick me with this meal. I think that this is how people live. I don't think that they even see what they are doing.

The problem is that the system works just enough to keep the hope alive.

After lunch, we're back on the bikes for the short ride to Kasengeshi.

## Sampwe, 1998

*A*t Mukana we could have turned right, east, to go to Sampwe. Sampwe is where I was in 1998 when the evacuation of all United Methodist missionaries was called. Sampwe is also where I learned how patronage is done.

In that year, the road between Mukana and Sampwe was repaired. The Grand Chief had crews of volunteers working on the sand road. It was smooth. The governor promised to visit.

In a patronage system, hospitality to the patron generates goodwill and favors. The governor would then grant the community needed resources. But the governor didn't come.

I was thinking that the same effort put into developing a working farm-to-market road would solve the region's poverty. Sampwe was a breadbasket. There were two crops of corn per year and three peanut crops, and rice is in the fields year-round. But the roads were so bad that all this produce fails to get to market. Why not go talk with the chief down the road and section by section get this road fixed? Instead, the community put all its efforts into impressing the patron, expecting him to fix its problems.

The district superintendent took me out to a field that he said had been walked off by the missionary pilot Stan Ridgeway twelve years before. Stan had remarked that this would make a good landing field. Stan was killed by government soldiers for refusing to fly a military mission, but the community still built the runway, ready for the next missionary to come.

Patronage and dependency are not the same thing. Clients in a patronage system are not lazy. They work hard. But their work is directed toward the patron, not their own progress.

The Grand Chief was a university-educated man. He spent most of his time in Lubumbashi in a fine house in the city. He was in Sampwe when we were there, so the district superintendent arranged for an audience.

Those were tense times. The war was coming, any day now. The Grand Chief's house was an armed camp, truckloads of soldiers surrounding the place. But the welcome was friendly.

We sat down with the Grand Chief to listen to his plans for community development. Nobody did patronage better than this chief did. He worked his patron, the governor, for what the community needed, and played the patron in the community, passing out resources and his constituents to work on projects. His project now was building a school. I watched as he played the Methodists against the Catholics in an honor/shame game to motivate us to build his dream school. Our district superintendent was equally skilled in the honor/shame game and got a commitment of 40,000 bricks from the chief. Well played.

# *Kasengeshi*

$\mathcal{W}$e arrive in Kasengeshi in the late afternoon to a more modest greeting that is also more choreographed and organized. It's not like Palm Sunday or MacArthur's return. I get the feeling that the village doesn't need a patron, but they want me to see their progress. They're showing off.

The pastor is friendly, but it is clear that this show is run by the director of education, who will be our host while we are here. He is a missionary of sorts, sent here by the bishop to build up the school. Unlike in the United States, United Methodist laypeople in the Congo are subject to the bishop's appointment—especially laypeople in the fields of education or medicine, whom the bishop may just send to a village to build a school or a clinic.

The house is rambling and under continuous construction, a patchwork of indoor spaces linked by open-air passageways. It's raining and dark when we arrive, and inside it takes awhile for my eyes to adjust to the light of the dim LED lamp whose batteries are on their last electrons. The ceiling is low and seems to get lower toward the back of the room, but it's actually the floor that rises, and piles of sand and rocks fill the back corners. A large wooden table is in the center of the room, and plastic chairs are placed around it for our sitting. I guess that my bedroom is the master bedroom as it has been in other villages, but getting to know our host, I think this one might actually be a purpose-built guest room. The floor is hard dirt. The bed is large. There's a small table beside the bed with a candle and a box of matches. The room is dark, even in the day, a wooden shutter closing the small glassless window against the rain, which has cooled everything. Everything is soaked. I zip off my pant legs, pull off my socks, and find a dry T-shirt.

Before the meal, a bath is offered. I'm led back through a hallway to the bathing room. The back of the house has no ceiling, so it feels like a rambling metal-roofed tent with small brick rooms along a maze of hallways. The shower room is a small unfinished cubby hole: half storage room, half a square burlap mat with a floor drain to the outside. A simple bedsheet with a SpongeBob design serves as the door. There are a bucket of warm water, a bar of soap, and a towel provided for my bathing. Feeling fresh and clean and drier, I return from my bath to find the table set. The meal is being brought out a bit at a time as it is prepared. Peanuts and bananas first.

The toilet is out back. I'm led through the rain, jumping small rivers of runoff between buildings of this complex house. The toilet itself is elevated and dry, but the doorframe has settled into an awkward shape, making the door difficult to open or, once opened, close. The floor is hardened dirt over tree branches with the appropriate hole. I balance my flashlight in a niche and, holding my breath and my pants, do the deed.

Back from my toilet call, I hang out on the small covered front porch to watch a young girl drawing water from the well, pulling up the bucket with a rope. She's washing clothes, even as it rains. In front of the house is a large community room that serves as a movie theater. An oversized satellite dish dominates the front yard. This is for showing World Cup football matches. A generator must be run for movies and games. I suspect that it's a rare occasion when all systems work. So many projects like this never work at all, or they work the day they are installed, then something breaks.

The rain sets in. It comes in cycles from hard downpour to light sprinkle. This continues for two days. If we get caught in the rain on the road, we continue, but we won't start in this rain. We need to get back on the road, but it is so inviting to hole up here.

## Kasengeshi to Mitwaba

On the third day of rain in Kasengeshi, I've lost complete sense of what day it is, or even of what day of the week it is, but we decide we're going today, even in the rain. By midmorning, the rain lets up enough for us to hit the road, and we're off again.

With the late morning start, it's going to take every bit of daylight available to reach our goal of riding at least 20 kilometers beyond Mitwaba before stopping for the day. We leave Kasengeshi with little fanfare, but with fresh legs. It feels good to be out on the road. It's still raining, gently. Eventually, the rain stops, but I don't notice when.

We're going uphill most of the day, but at a grade that is almost unnoticed. We gradually climb for most of the morning. The last 10 kilometers into Mitwaba are back downhill, again not at a really noticeable grade, but we're getting a little pull from gravity. The road into Mitwaba is busy with bicycles. It is wide, but it's a rocky mess with rambling deep ruts left by the trucks that allow for only one good track. Downhill runaway bikes loaded with charcoal have the right of way.

Just inside the town limits, I pull my bike under one of the eucalyptus trees that line the wide main street. Mulongo and the Mitwaba district superintendent go on ahead to find the church's greeting party. I wait and rest in the shade. Children gather to watch me.

Mitwaba is a different kind of town, an up-country mountain mining town. It's the Wild West. The Congo I've been exposed to is a hyperreligious country. This town is not. I've spent all my time in the Congo safely cradled inside the church, which has given me a skewed impression of the influence the church has on society. We've now entered an unchurched town.

We're escorted by a couple of local motorcycles through town. The first official building we come to is the United Nations Peacekeeping outpost. It's a small post. We see only one white truck and three uniformed soldiers. The UN soldiers look like stragglers left behind when the main force moved north. One guy looks too old for this work, as old as I am. We exchange greetings and take posed photos.

Two things stand out to me in Mitwaba: the number of motorcycles and the number of men smoking. Motorcycles and cigarettes are sure signs of discretionary income, cash on hand—too much cash, maybe. We pass bars and movie houses. These are rough-looking places, made mostly of scrap construction materials, sheets of tin, and orange tarps. It takes little imagination to conclude that prostitution and AIDS are behind those doors.

The congregation in Mitwaba wants us to accept its hospitality for the night. Our refusal is politically and socially difficult, but we need to go beyond Mitwaba today in order to get a head start on the mountain crossing tomorrow. We do accept the hospitality of a meal and a warm bucket of water for bathing. There is plenty of time while the meal is prepared. I take the first turn inside the grass-paneled shower stall for a bucket bath.

After we all bathe, we're taken for a walk around town to see where the congregation worships and the plot of land that has been purchased for the building of a new church. There is surprisingly open talk about the conflicts, both internal and external, that are holding the church back. The United Methodist congregation in Mitwaba meets in one of those bar/movie theaters. The members have acquired the land to build a proper church, but things are not going well. This is a hard town to start a church in.

The district superintendent explains to us that although this is called the Mitwaba District of The United Methodist Church, it has had trouble getting a congregation started here. Even the district superintendent's home is in Sampwe; the one attempt to move the district parsonage to Mitwaba was a failure.

After three hours in Mitwaba, Mulongo is eager to get back on the road and get in as much distance as possible before dark.

Passing out of town, we see the ruins of the old British Brethren mission hospital. At one time, Mitwaba had an excellent hospital. It's no wonder that many locals want the missionaries to return. There is no denying that things have gone from bad to worse since the missionaries left Mitwaba, and there's no sign of things turning around. This reality pushes back against everything I think I know about the importance of local control. This is what keeps my brain spinning.

There's a gradual downhill run out of Mitwaba for maybe the first hour. It's rocky, on the edge of challenging. When we're still above 4,000 feet, the road levels out and turns to red sand as it weaves through tall grass and a few small, scrubby trees.

We come to a fork in the road that has created a small village. The right fork leads into the bush, and we take the left fork without stopping or even slowing down. This is not a village to spend any time in.

Even for Congolese, this village has a deadly reputation. There is a tick that lives in the grass at this peculiar elevation, and only this elevation, that is deadly to all, even the local residents. I had been warned by missionary John Enright to never sleep under grass roofs in the mountains because of this tick. His warning had made me fear sleeping in any grass-roofed hut. Now I'm traveling through the village famous for this tick, and Mulongo is determined not to spend any time there. It was actually liberating, to go from a general fear of all grass-roofed huts to possessing the knowledge of this particular threat. Know your enemy.

After a couple more hours of riding, we find a village where we can spend the night. The village United Methodist church is a small mud-and-grass hut with goats in it. We pitch our tents inside and share the space with the goats.

## Mother and Child

*I*n the morning we pack up early and get on the road. There's no time to waste. This crossing must be made in a day. It can't be divided in half. We're facing Mount Mulumbi, the Mother of Mountains. In the local mythology, this is the mountain that birthed all the other mountains. I, of course, am hearing, "Tomorrow we cross Mount Mulumbi, and it's a Mother." Actually, we have been climbing this mountain for the last three days, and there's not that much of a climb left. It's not a mountain as you think of a mountain, peaks and all, but rather a high plateau that ends in this grand escarpment with two major descents: first the Child, then the Mother. We are going over the cliff, and it's the descent that's going to kill us.

There will be no church visits today. In a way, this is a break. The receiving end of hospitality can wear you down. It will be good for the team to do nothing but team things today, even if they are hard team things.

The road before us is beautiful, stretching out in a tiny red ribbon crossing a green valley. You can make out a river down below and something that looks like maybe a bridge. Then the red ribbon snakes up and away from the river, and disappears into the next rise. The morning is damp with mist. That's good. Let the sun take its time getting up. Cool wet air on my face, eyes watering, and nose running, but this is good riding, typical of the mornings.

The road around the bridge is all washed out and difficult, consuming all energy that we have built in the downhill run, but once we've climbed out of the riverbed, the road improves to passable. And the climb begins.

Even the strain of pushing a loaded bicycle up the countless switchbacks of a mountain road doesn't cause me to miss the roadside waterfalls and stunning vistas. I point out the beauty of the land. Shabana confesses that he and others who ride this road are so immersed in their misery that they fail to see the beauty. He begins to reflect on the beauty of the country as an unclaimed asset: "Even though we live in poverty, we must not miss the beauty."

As we approach the summit, the vista opportunities are lost. It's as if we're going into the mountain. It's all rock walls and waterfalls.

Midday the road levels out and we ride a ridge along the side of the mountain. The road is more of a rocky riverbed. Water runs down from above and washes the road out, down to its bedrock. This is technical riding up and down over slick, sharp limestone slabs. Pick a line. I try to stay on the bike and not walk it any more than absolutely necessary. This is where my teammates shame me. They appear to be fearless on these rocks, staying on their bikes while I finally have to get off and walk.

I miss the summit. At some point, we make the transition from climb to descent. After surviving the Child, we're only a third of the way down.

We break out of the mountain forest facing the other side of the world. We stop in a well-worn pulloff. Even though we are the only ones here at this time, it has all the evidence of being a busy place. Soldiers have used one of the trees as target practice. It is riddled with bullets in a gross way that leads one to imagine a night of undisciplined, drug-induced excess of automatic rifle fire. This was—is still—a crazy war fought by out-of-control soldiers.

This spot is strategically important. From it you can see all movement on the only road that crosses the mountains to the south. An army threatening Lubumbashi has to cross here. General Patton would have loved to stand on this site, overlooking the valley, and imagine the movement of troops below. A concrete artillery emplacement is just a few clicks up the ridge. It commands the whole valley below. Back when I was a kid playing army, we called it a *pillbox*.

But the coolest thing about this spot is the sign. It's in Swahili, and it says, "Ring the bell before descending." A truck wheel rim hanging from a pole frame is the bell, and you strike it with an iron rod. I have to have a picture of my bike leaning against this sign. This spot will become my most favorite photo stop in the entire world. There's a man in the village 3,000 feet below whose job it is to hear the bell and answer with his bell when the traffic is clear for you to descend the mountain. The road down is too narrow for two-way traffic. It's not a big deal to us on bicycle, but the big transports have to wait.

We ring the bell and wait for the response, then we start down.

Frank, my bicycle mechanic at Bicycle Garage Indy—the one who built my wheels and prepped the bike with spare spokes that are taped to the front rack, spare chain links, spare brake and shifting cables, and a bag of bits and bolts—assured me that in a 600-mile ride, I was not going to need replacement brake pads. He was wrong. I am absolutely burning up a set of brake pads on this descent.

Not only that, but my hands don't have the reach or the grip strength to control the brake levers on the drop bars. I am running out of brake pads *and* grip strength on the way down. I have found my personal threshold of adventure. On one hand, invigorating; on the other, I'm beginning to realize the very real possibilities that this descent is presenting.

First of all, I'm afraid of the shame of falling. I understand shame. I understand living with the twin motivators of honor and shame. Shame is a much greater fear for me than any physical threat.

My second fear of falling is the fear of breaking my bicycle. There are parts that can't be fixed if broken. There are parts that I can't fix if they break. That's a pragmatic problem, as well as a shame issue.

Down the list is my fear of breaking an arm. For some reason, I don't fear breaking a leg. I guess that's because the panniers would act as big air bags in the event of a fall and protect my legs, or at least my mind thinks they would do that. Anyway, break an arm here, though, and we're days from medical help. Of course, we don't wear helmets. Guess I should worry about head injuries.

Not on the worry list is falling to my death. First, it's no worry because that solves all problems. Second, even though my wife is convinced that I am determined to die in Africa and be buried here, I don't believe I will. My gut tells me that I will die of old age in Indiana, or maybe Florida, whilst telling stories of Africa to my great-grandchildren.

The distance from the bell down to the floor of the mountain is maybe 3,000 feet. Most of the ride is good rolling, smooth enough and safe enough. Then come the sharp rocks where the water moving from one waterfall to the next runs over the road. I can't see the falls themselves, but I can hear them. It's pleasant, cool, and shady, just a bit of dampness to the air. The road is almost a tunnel through the forest, a wall on the upside and dense bush and treetops on the downside. Only occasionally does the view open up to the world below. When it does, I have to stop just to catch my breath. I see a tiny village and farm fields, surrounded by forests and grass in a patchwork of many shades of green. I take a picture, knowing that the photo will come out flat and have none of the depth of field needed to capture this panorama.

When the road gets too steep and the rocks too treacherous for me, I get off and walk. I'm amazed at the recklessness of my colleagues. They free-fall down this mountain with what amounts to no brakes. I'm going to try to keep up. Back on the bike, I let the brakes go open and instantly pick up speed. This is much steeper than it looks. Now I'm going too fast for my comfort, and the bike is out of my control. I can only pick a track over the limestone slabs and live or die with that choice. The rocks are flat and slick in places, and sharp and sticking straight up in other places. I aim through the gaps of the sharp rocks and hold my breath on the flat, slick rocks, knowing that one wrong turn of the handlebars will send the wheels flying over my head, flipping the whole show upside down. This is fast and scary, and unlike the roller coaster rides at Kings Island, this is for real.

The rocks are now coming at me too fast for good decisions. I dodge one but can't avoid the next. Then comes a whole row of jagged rocks—no, two rows, three rows, all the way across the road. I can only hang on and try to keep the bike upright. Boom! Boom! Double blowout. Both tires are cut by the rocks and I'm on two flats. The mountain is still pulling me down and I don't have enough brake to stop the bike. I ride the tires to shreds, and when the bike finally slows, I'm still upright.

Éléphant arrives and takes the bike from me. As long as he's around, he's the mechanic, so I sit on the side of the road and catch my breath. The tubes are shreds and the tires are cut, but the rims are still round. Probably the decision to keep the bike headed straight into the rock ledges instead of turning saved the rims as it sacrificed the tires. For now, we replace them with the two spares I'm carrying. This is it. After this there are no more spares. I have lots of tubes, but just two spare tires. Éléphant will sew up the tires later. Most bikes (and motorcycles) on this road are riding on patched and sewn tires.

We're off again, but I'm even more cautious. The others will just have to wait for me at the bottom of the mountain. I'm walking down. When they are too far ahead, I try to ride again. I hop back up on the bike, and with hands gripping the brakes, I pick my way over the rocks, avoiding the tire cutters. "*Pole pole, pole pole,*" I say to myself in Swahili, "slowly, slowly."

As I get more comfortable, I let off the brakes and pick up speed. I'm riding again. The road's not bad. This is good.

Around another corner, I meet rocks again. Shit! I brake and steer to miss the worst but fail. The panniers protect my legs as I go down, but the mountain doesn't stop. You'd think that once you hit the ground, the fall is over, but it's not. I keep rolling and sliding, and it's all in slow motion.

There's no one around. If a tree falls in the forest and there's no one around to hear it, does it make a noise? If a *mzungu* falls in the forest, and there is no one around to see it, is there shame? I get up, but the bike doesn't want to be picked up and flops awkwardly, the weight of the front panniers turning the front wheel and the weight of the rear panniers refusing to get up. I jerk the bike as if it would understand my frustration with its behavior. Right now, this feels like a bad day on a bicycle.

The great thing about a long day on a bicycle riding down a mountain, though, is that it's a long day on a bicycle riding down a mountain. Nothing is broken, on me or the bicycle. I'm in Africa at a place no other American has had the opportunity to be, and I'm here because I'm pretty much the only person, American or Congolese, who thinks this is the most amazing place on earth. One look across the valley below, and I'm over my frustration with the bike and the mountain, and, for a moment, at one with the universe. Right now, there is no purpose for this mission other than to be here in this moment "when peace, like a river, attendeth my way."[1]

Eventually the bike decides to cooperate again, and I continue. At the floor of the mountain, we hit a muddy, two-track road that carries us across a swamp and a concrete bridge. Before sunset, we arrive at the village of Ntambo, home to the bell that answers the bell at the beginning of the descent. We meet with the man responsible for answering the bell, take photos, and joke around.

Mulongo goes to find us a place to sleep and comes back with a young man who guides us to the chief's house. I have been briefed and know the protocol, but still I forget to remove my Red Sox baseball cap when entering the stick fence that surrounds the chief's yard. I'm embarrassed to be caught in such a stupid tourist faux pas. I hate being seen as a tourist even though there haven't been tourists here for two generations now.

The chief greets us and introduces us to his family. He invites us to take photos. The most powerful man in this village lives in a grass-roofed hut with a front yard filled with chickens. He has his dignity, but not much else to speak of, even by Congolese standards. We pitch our tents in the chief's front yard and spend the evening in food preparation and bicycle maintenance.

In the morning, we're off early to cross the plateau before our next descent. Through the early morning hours, until the sun cooks each day dry, my nose runs. It runs freely, making yellow elevens on my face. And my eyes water, which is a problem I've had since I was a teenager. At the U.S. Naval Academy, the doctor determined that the tear ducts that drain my eyes are clogged. He tried to lance them open.

"Tell me when you can taste this," he said as he put drops in my eyes. Apparently, the tear ducts drain into the back of the mouth. Who knew? He lanced until I could taste it. Then a week later the ducts closed again, and that was the last attempt at correcting the problem.

I just live with it. In the morning, my eyes water, and tears stream down my face. For me, the drain just doesn't work. It can be embarrassing, coming into an impor-

---

[1] "It Is Well with My Soul." Words by Horatio G. Spafford, 1873. Music by Philip P. Bliss, 1876. *The United Methodist Hymnal*. Nashville, TN: The United Methodist Publishing House, 1989, no. 377.

tant meeting early in the morning with tears running down my cheeks, and in the winter, my face can freeze, which is not pleasant. But mostly, I've managed to avoid winter, and serving in the Congo helps with that.

Now every morning, my eyes are watering and my nose is running, and I've finally stopped trying to fix the problem. I'm probably known from village to village as the missionary with the running nose. After weeks of riding with a running nose, it dawns on me that the irritant might be the sunscreen on my forehead running down into my eyes and around my nose. Maybe it is that cheap drugstore generic brand I saved so much money on, or maybe it's any sunscreen, but on the road in the Congo, you can come to regret not spending a bit more and buying a quality product.

Product placement time: Unlike my questionable sunscreen, my Merrell hiking boots are perfect. I didn't intend to pay $80 for a pair of shoes, but I couldn't find anything at my price point that matched what I was looking for. They're summer-weight, so they stay cooler and dry out faster. They're also high tops, to protect the ankles from flying pedals. The treads grip the studs on the BMX pedals while riding, and off the bike they're perfect for mud, sand, rocks, climbing, descending, walking all day. Great shoes.

We pass through a village that has some development going on, and a sign indicates that it's a rehabilitation and resettlement project for internally displaced persons following the war. There are about half a dozen brick water stations with taps fed by a mountain spring spread over about a kilometer. And there is a well-built school that looks like new construction. Why this kind of development happens in one place and not another is a mystery. This is not a big village, and there are not very many people around. The children must be in school, and the men must be in the fields. Don't know where the women are. Reminds me of the Gospel story of Jesus and the woman at the well. Guess this isn't the time of day for gathering water. One young mother with her baby wrapped close to her stands quietly by herself, and she allows me to take her picture.

# Rest Stop

*M*y rhythm isn't matching Mulongo's. I want to ride faster, but I need frequent rest stops. His pace is too slow for me, but he never stops. Maybe I'm showing my age. Then again, even in my peak performance days, I was never good at rhythm. As a swimmer, I could not get comfortable with the breathing. On the track, I was too slow to be a good sprinter. My coach tried to make me a distance runner, but I just could not get the rhythm of long distance running.

I've taken advantage of the speed of my bike and gone out ahead of the team. I'm not leading, just running ahead. On this stretch, you can count on a small village popping up about every 5 kilometers or so in predictable places: on the top of the hill to protect the village from flooding, but not too far from water. Cross a stream, head uphill, and expect to find a village. This is hot riding, so I stop to rest under a tree in a small village and watch a chicken peck at the ground next to me.

The forest along the road is pretty scrubby; there has been a lot of deforestation. Charcoal is the primary cooking and heating fuel, but the climate doesn't seem to want to grow big trees. A baobab is a rare sight, but a stand of mature palm, banana, and eucalyptus trees on the road ahead means that you're looking at a village under those trees.

The eucalyptus was brought by the railroad a hundred years ago for railroad ties. Termites ate all the eucalyptus ties, so now all the railroad ties are made of steel, and stands of eucalyptus trees around towns and villages provide shade.

I've ridden ahead and am resting under a tree. One day in a village, I remarked on the beauty of the tree-lined main street. Mulongo told me a story his grandfather had told him: Under the Belgians, trees were planted along the roads, one in front of each hut. The health of that tree was the responsibility of the family who lived in that hut. If the tree died, the family members were beaten so severely that families chose to abandon their homes and flee into the bush if the trees in front of their huts died. It may be a long time before these people have positive feelings toward trees, especially trees that white men bring. Any aid group contemplating a reforestation program should know this history.

The rest of the team comes around the bend and up the hill. This is a good day, no real problems. I just get back on the bike and ride.

# On to Kyolo

*T*oday is a long day on the bike, and the road is stretching out in front of us. At a distance the road looks fine, but up close it is slow going up and down steep hills. Fourteen kilometers per hour is our top speed on the open road today.

There it is: the red eleven. Looking ahead, the road seems to go straight up to heaven in a double band of red. I gear down to the next to the lowest gear I have, then to the lowest, and settle in for a long, slow climb. Behind me the others have already started to walk their bikes up the hill, then push them.

I'm feeling strong and know that I'm going to top this hill successfully. As it peaks and levels, the road bends around to the left and there it is—more hill, steeper yet. And the red clay-sand gives way to rock. There is already water streaming down the road, crossing from side to side. It's starting to rain.

No way can I ride this: too steep, too rocky, too slippery. I'm off the bike pushing, and the pushing is hard, the bike heavy, the road steep. I'm at the limit of my strength. Then, down the road from way above, he comes: Éléphant in his rubber waders is stomping down the hill toward me and wearing a big smile.

He takes my bike and starts pushing it up the hill. I follow. There's no need to fight it. Éléphant has decided that his job is to carry my bike across water and push it up hills. I'll have to prove my manhood in some other way. Halfway up the next switchback, we pass his motorcycle. He'll push my bike as far as necessary, then come back for it.

The rain comes and goes. Sometimes I don't even notice it. It pours for a half hour, then slows, then stops. Other than reducing visibility and making the rocks more slippery than they already are, it really doesn't really slow us down.

Éléphant has gone back to his motorcycle and I'm back to pushing my own bike. It's too rocky to ride. The road is more of a creek bed. I push on around another bend.

Waterfalls are so common that I've quit looking up when I hear the roar of water. Nevertheless, I stop at a small falls coming out of the side of the mountain because it is a good place to wait for the others to catch up.

They're not far behind, and we enjoy the refreshing water. An hour ago, we were soaked in the rain. Now that we've been dried in the sun, the water feels good again. I take off my Red Sox cap, fill it in the falling water, and cool my head. The team drinks freely from the stream. I'm not confident on the safety of this water, although it is just minutes from being in the clouds and nowhere near people or animals. I pass on drinking.

Together, we top the climb and find the high plateau. I know this is not Everest or even the Rockies, but we're now on the top of the world, it seems. Ahead, the plateau goes on to the horizon. To the left and right, the land drops off into deep valleys. We're looking across the valleys at mountaintops, and we're level with the mountaintops.

Now the road is barely a trace, but it is smooth and only occasionally presents obstacles. We ride at a comfortably fast pace. The air is fresh, even cool, at this altitude. The sky is partly cloudy, hiding the intense sun.

This is lion country, or it used to be lion country. During the war, the big wild animals, including the lions, were killed or driven deeper into the mountain sanctuaries. Mulongo assures me that there are still lions, but they're deep in the forest nowadays. With the sun setting on these jagged rock formations cropping out of the high grasses, I'm aware of how far off the tourist path we are, and how magical a place this is.

The sun has set on us and we don't have a place to stay. The next village is 10 kilometers away. That's another hour.

My mind wanders back to where I left off in my tutorial on the Process.

# Listening and Language

*W*hen you hit a generative theme, the room comes alive. If you get it wrong and try to feed back a code that doesn't hit a generative theme, it falls flat. This is not a problem. When your code falls flat, move on. Go back around again and try something else. It's not about you, and it doesn't revolve around your brilliance. You don't have to understand. You don't have to solve the problem. You can't solve the problem.

Which brings up another point: How is it that I can do this listening when I don't know the language people are speaking? This is going to be the most controversial and counterlogical piece of the puzzle, yet it may be the key to my success, counterlogically speaking.

The conventional wisdom, passed down for generations, is that a missionary must first learn the language of the people. How obvious is that? Learning the language is the first step in getting to know the people. How can you communicate if you don't learn the language? I don't know enough French to get safely through the airport, and yet I make it through the airport. Most of the Swahili I learned back in the 1990s was quickly forgotten. I get excited when I recognize a word that I remember. But even if I could speak French and Swahili, these languages would not help me with listening in the villages. Kiluba is the language of the villages. Congolese go to school to learn French, and even Swahili is not a first language for anyone around here, not like in Kenya or Tanzania.

I know maybe three words in Kiluba.

How does that work then, these listening sessions? Not knowing the language is a handicap, but it's a handicap that pushes me to a different level of listening. Not knowing the language makes no sense to the outside observer. It makes no sense to any other missionary or aid worker. It also frustrates the people I come to work with, and that is just the point.

Here's the flip side: Learning the language makes sense if I'm the one who is going to solve the problem, if I'm going to process all of the facts and craft a workable answer. But I'm not the one who has to solve the problem. The community has to solve this, and my job is to provoke the community into solving its own problems. Frustrating the villagers by not being able to speak the language is one way to provoke them. It confuses them. It destabilizes the conversation. It removes a comfortable arrangement and substitutes something nobody knows what to do with. I'm not available to them as an answer. You see, it doesn't matter that I don't understand what is being said; it matters that they work the Process. I'm here to facilitate a problem-solving exercise. I am not the problem solver.

I can see David Hilton back in 1997, sitting there, leading our group in Atlanta, saying almost nothing. A few words telling us what to do, but never explaining what we are doing. We had to figure out that ourselves. The Zen master leading his disciples with an economy of commands. Wax on, wax off. On one hand, he knew where we were going, where he was taking us, but on the other hand, he didn't care where we were going, That was not up to him; it was up to us.

Communication is much more than speaking words. Listening is much more than hearing words. It can go much deeper than that. Not knowing the words creates an opportunity to go to a deeper place of knowing. First, because I cannot speak, I cannot talk. I must be quiet and listen. Second, because I cannot understand the words, the people speaking to me cannot deceive me with their words—not that they mean to lie to me, but they are repeating lies that have been taught them. This kind of listening is both exhausting and liberating at the same time. It also takes weeks, months. This is why I take the long route, ride a bicycle. Time must be slowed until it is virtually standing still. There are times in the middle of these long bicycle trips that time does stand still and I think that I can see eternity, both directions.

It's not that I don't understand anything that is being said. It's amazing that even when you don't know the words, you know what's being said. I hear clearly this feeling of abandonment. I hear hope and hopelessness in the same sentence. I am at the beginning of understanding a community that continues to expect a broken system to deliver the help it so desperately needs. The details are bad water, killer diseases, lack of education. Underneath are assumed promises, imagined relationships, trust misplaced. There is also much that I am hearing that is outside my range of hearing, like a dog whistle. It will never come to my conscious understanding, but it will yet shape what I am thinking.

My observation is that most people seem to learn a language in order to tell someone else what they think that person needs to know. Few, if any, learn a language in order to hear what the other person has to say. Don't believe me? My good friend David Livingstone was nearly sacked by the London Missionary Society for the heresy of heterodoxy, the appreciation that the others might have some understanding of God and the universe and theology that you could learn from them. He was about to be brought up on charges, but he managed to jump ship to the Royal

Geographical Society before the good church folk could fire him. Missionaries go to exotic places to preach to strange people what the missionaries know to be the truth, with no thought that the folks to whom they are preaching might have a whole rich theological tradition worth learning about and from.

I think that someday I want to learn Kiluba, but if I do, it will come from the listening side, not the telling side.

This thing with not knowing the language is a part of a larger conviction that it is not the mistakes we have made that have gotten us to where we are. It has been our best practices. In the short run, we can blame a few bad actors or ineffective leaders, but over time, and missionaries have been in the Congo for more than 100 years, we arrive at the place we have been headed toward intentionally. Therefore, as my logic goes, if we are not happy with where we are—and I'm not happy, and don't think anyone in the Congo thinks that we are in a good place—then it is not the mistakes that we have made, but our so-called best practices that need to be questioned. So I question everything and turn everything upside down. If the collective wisdom has been to learn the language first, I'll learn the language last. Why? Simple. Learning the language first got us to where we are. No need to repeat that. I'll do it backwards. It can't hurt because everything is already broken. I can't break it any more. We must experiment with models that are exactly the opposite of what we've believed to have worked, or rather what we have believed should work. We must question everything, especially everything that we have come to believe as true.

# *Fork in the Road*

*W*e spend the night in Kyolo, where there's an abbreviated worship and greetings. Our program has shifted from district visits to getting to Mulongo. In the morning, before the sun is up, we're ready to get on the road; we are like horses that have caught the smell of the barn. Our departure is delayed, though, when word comes that the chief wants to see us before we leave town. We can't know how long we will wait for the Grand Chief to receive us, but this is not an invitation we can decline. There aren't too many rules out here, but when the chief says he wants to see you, you go see the chief.

The Grand Chief's house is a gated compound with a concrete block wall and a large steel gate. It's not fancy—more like what you might see around an industrial yard back home—but it is formidable. We are let in through the smaller pedestrian door and taken to a chief-sized pavilion to await the appearance of the Grand Chief.

We wait. Around the compound are trucks and tractors in various states of disrepair. There are several small outbuildings, storage sheds, and apartments for extended family and staff. From where we are sitting, I can't get a good look at the Grand Chief's house, nor will I. We won't be invited in.

The Grand Chief arrives. He's as friendly as can be, making us feel welcome and important to him. I have no doubt that this welcome is genuine. He exudes joy. Despite the armed guards with him, there is no intimidation, and I feel no threat. His greetings do not emphasize welcoming a white person; our United Methodist team is important to him, and Mulongo is getting as much attention as I am.

He tells me that he was the first United Methodist convert, a friend of Bishop Booth, who was the last white bishop. He compliments me by telling me that I remind him of Bishop Booth. I'm flattered because Bishop Booth is known for his commitment to turning over leadership to Congolese church leaders, and I understand my task as completing his unfinished work. The more I learn about some of the early missionaries, the more I'm impressed with how progressive and almost outlaw they were.

Mulongo presents the chief with one of the inexpensive watches he had asked me to buy and bring along, the kind you get in the jewelry section at a big-box store for $10 or $12. The chief goes to the house and comes back with a couple of small plastic bags of ore and gives them to us. One has tin and the other coltan.

We get an upbeat lecture on development from the Grand Chief. Once again, I'm impressed. He's well-read and knows as much as anyone about how prosperity could be brought to his people. He tells me that he has seen on the Internet a machine that can dig and sift gold out of the riverbed. Am I aware of this machine? Can I get him one?

Then he lays upon me a proposal that is well beyond my imagining. Can we partner together to form a mining company that will be able to put the proceeds back into the community, a community mining company that funds needed infrastructure and schools and clean water and health care?

This is the first time, but not the last time, that we will be invited to such an adventure. I am rightfully afraid of such a deal in the cutthroat mining business. There is no shortage of warlords, criminals, and invading foreign armies who would not hesitate to cut off our heads for venturing into their business. Then there is the government, which would squish us like a bug if we dared get into mining. And how could we compete with the multinational mining companies?

The idea doesn't go away, though. The right chief, one really interested in community development, strong enough to deal with the government, and powerful enough to fend off the warlords, could perhaps make it work. I'm trying to keep a level head about this and not get sucked into the gold fever, but before this expedition is over, we will know more about local politics than just about any outsider. We might just be able to operate under the radar of the big mining companies and pick up what they are not interested in. It's too tempting, too scary.

The visit with the Grand Chief put us behind, but by midmorning, we've arrived at an open-air market, and we're ready for a rest. The market consists of one row of booths constructed of sticks and grass lining the road. On one side is a brick-and-stucco storefront that looks closed. The roadside market offers essentials: toiletries, tins of sardines, and warm Coca-Cola in cans only. I do miss the bottles. The others buy some locally prepared *bukari* in a banana leaf. I get a packet of shortbread cookies. We sit in bamboo chairs under a low grass canopy with our food and Fantas for each of us. We're the kings of cool until I stumble getting out of the bamboo chair and hit my head on the low grass canopy, spilling the Fanta all over myself.

This market sits at a fork in the road—the only decision to be made in more than 300 kilometers. One side goes to Mulongo, the other to Manono. We'll take the road to Mulongo.

# Manono, 1995

*M*anono is not in the plan this year, but I remember Manono from 1995 when the Tanganyika-Tanzania Annual Conference meeting was held there. In the interim between Bishop wa Kadilo's death and the election of a new bishop for North Shaba (now called North Katanga), Bishop Katembo from the Southern Zaire Conference was presiding. Ntambo Nkulu, not yet elected bishop, was my handler and translator.

We flew into Manono from Lubumbashi. I had only planned to speak at the conference in Nyembo Mpungu the week before, but that had gone so well that Bishop Katembo insisted I stay and preach the same sermons in Manono. He said, "You understand our issues." I tried to modestly protest, but he pushed the point, saying that they had had missionaries who had been there 30 years who didn't understand them.

I actually thought that I did understand their issues. Even John Enright said to me one day, on the eve of my departure in 1999, in front of another missionary who was horrified by how John opened the discussion, "You know what I hate about you, Bob? . . . You came off the plane asking the questions that took me all these years to figure out." This seemed odd because I sure don't get the issues in American churches.

In total blind obedience to Bishop Katembo, I turned over my passport and airline tickets to the conference staff for the necessary arrangements. In addition, I turned over the three teenagers who were traveling with me, including my daughter, Taylor, to the same conference staff, who assured me that the children would be escorted safely to the airport and put on the plane for America. As it happened, they missed their plane in Lubumbashi, and Tampouse, the bishop's driver, desperately drove them through the night to Lusaka to catch the British Airways flight to London. In the middle of not understanding the languages and totally outplayed in the honor/shame game, I was helpless myself and useless to my charges. That's the most irresponsible thing I have ever done in my life.

The Southern Zaire Wings of the Morning missionary pilot dropped Ntambo Nkulu and me off at the Manono airstrip. At one time this had been an active airport, but all that was left in 1995 was the grass strip and an abandoned terminal. A stake-bed truck met us there.

This was the same truck that had met us at this airstrip in 1991, when I came to Manono with a delegation from Indiana in the Congo to visit missionary families. As an extra treat, we were taken to see a Pygmy[2] village in the forest around Manono. A little green spot on the Michelin map indicated rain forest, but in the dry season the forest was mostly scrub trees and brownish-gray grass. We were ill-prepared to walk for a couple of hours in the hot sun with very little shade. There was no promise that we would find the Pygmies, who are nomadic and might have relocated since the missionaries had seen them last. An evangelism outreach had been begun with them, however, and we were being taken to see this novel group of people.

Pygmy villages are no more than bark lean-tos along the trail, and we might have walked right through this village and missed them, but they were there to greet us. They were not as small as I had expected, but certainly they were a different people group than the Bantu. I think that there is as big a culture gap between Pygmies and Bantu as there is between Bantu and Europeans. A Pygmy on a downtown street in Lubumbashi would be more out of place than a Bantu walking down the sidewalk of London.

We had a great time together. The Pygmy men showed us the bows and poisoned arrows they used to hunt small game. We all worshiped under a large baobab tree, singing songs and praying. It required two translators to bridge the language gap: Twa to Kiluba, Kiluba to English. It was truly a once-in-a-lifetime experience of the sort few Americans ever have the opportunity to enjoy. It was a David Livingstone sort of day worth remembering. But that's enough about 1991.

In 1995, on the third day of conference, I was taken back out to see the Pygmy village. This time we had no trouble finding it because the villagers had settled permanently by building a red brick United Methodist church as their Bantu pastor had instructed. The Pygmies were proud and excited to show us their church, a short building with walls of handmade bricks under a grass roof. We entered almost on our knees, and when I stood up my head was in the rafters, and I'm only 5'9". There was no furniture but a stick pulpit and a stick chair for the visiting preacher; everyone else sat on the dirt floor. A mother nursed her infant while leaning through an open window to listen.

---

[2] The term *Pygmy* may be pejorative—I'm not certain—but I figure that if I use the terms *Twa* or *Bambenga* or *Bayaka,* you won't connect these people with the image in your mind. Both white missionaries and Congolese locals use the term *Pygmy*. Pygmies probably don't.

The Pygmies were in full celebration mode, with singing, dancing, and gifts to mark my visit, a chicken and a ceremonial ax (tomahawk-like). I preached on the parable of the treasure found in the field, doing my best to find something from the Gospels that might apply to their lives. Mostly, I simply enjoyed their hospitality, but I wept on the inside.

I couldn't get over the crushing realization that I was witnessing and participating in the end of one of the last true hunter-gatherer groups on the planet. After 13,000 years of nomadic life, the Pygmy village had located and built a brick community building. I couldn't help but imagine that in the next several years, we would be back to install electricity for their washing machines. Maybe it was going to happen with or without my participation, but it was still a sad experience. How much of their unique knowledge had we destroyed because we were in a hurry to teach them? How much could we have learned from them?

On the whole, though, my time in Manono in 1995 was rich in learning. The conference opened with a Sunday morning worship that was fun and filled with enthusiasm. We sang hymns I knew, although in a language I did not know. Everyone was involved in the singing and dancing, and homemade guitars and amps run off car batteries fascinated me. Choirs competed for the approval of the congregation with anthems that were created by each choir director out of Scripture stories. The youth choir did a long set that got everybody out of their seats and dancing. At the climax of one of the youth's songs, it began to snow. It was 103 degrees Fahrenheit in the shade and snowing! I looked up into the rafters and saw the coffee cans rigged to dump confetti when the concealed strings were pulled. Delightful! Funny! Joyous! Gotta love this level of unbridled worship.

After worship, chairs were set in a circle under a shade tree. This was the young adult time with the visiting missionary. One young man practicing his pretty good English asked the question of the day: "What will you tell the people in America about our village?"

I was stumped. When Ntambo and I flew in, we saw an abandoned airport terminal. We saw what had been a tree-lined boulevard that was now potholes, with most of the trees cut for firewood and weeds instead of groomed grass. We saw a business district boarded up. We were staying in a grand, old, run-down colonial house without electricity or running water. We saw a ghost town whose mine had closed a generation ago.

Quickly thinking, I turned the question back to the youth: "What do you want me to tell the people in America about your village?"

The young man spoke for the group. He told me about the houses in his village, their neat fence rows, the orderliness of their streets and blocks. He told me what his father did for work and about his mother's busy day. He told me about his school and the health center. All of these things he told me with pride. He was bragging about his village. He did not want me to tell people in America about how pathetic and desperate his life was. He wanted Americans to think things were fine and getting better.

When he was finished, one of his friends corrected him, "You didn't tell about the European section."

"Oh, that's dead." He dismissed it with a wave of his hand back over his shoulder.

The young man showed me a picture of a thriving African village when I had seen only the dead European section. Unfortunately, I was not the only one with impaired vision. Too many of the older Congolese church leaders were fixated on the dead European section and saw only a vision of the future that included its resurrection. The past defined their future. This young man and his friends saw a picture of the future that had no connection with the colonial past.

In 2005 Taylor accompanied Bishop Ntambo on a visit to Manono, his first visit to the village after the war. They found the churches in ruins along with most of the village. I wonder if the young man with the wonderful vision of the future of his village survived the war and, if so, what he is doing and seeing now.

# From the Fork to Mulongo

*I* hate sand! In the sand, my Cannondale is a liability—so much so that it is an embarrassment. The skinny tires cut right into the soft sand and I'm buried. Stopped cold, I can't even get in a short run before falling over. This is beyond embarrassment. It's humiliation. The others power on through, and I am shamed.

The road is now nothing but sand, the kind of sand on the dry part of the beach, not the hard-packed sand, the soft deep sand. Even pushing the bike is hard, and I'm not doing any reflecting or daydreaming on this stretch. I'm busy fighting my bicycle and cursing the sand. I get the opportunity to learn the name for sand in three new languages, and I curse it in all three, as well as in English.

When I take the time to look up from the sand, though, the landscape has changed a bit, ever so subtly. In an African sort of way, it is more residential. It's not urban, but a kind of long road of houses and yards. There's a lot of shade along this road, and the temperature has moderated to a comfortable cool—well, not quite cool, but not sticky hot. With effort, I can work up a sweat, but it takes effort. I suspect that this has something to do with why the road has become sand.

About 10 kilometers from our rest stop at the fork in the road, Mulongo announces that we are now in the Mulongo District. In another 5 kilometers, we pull into a village churchyard. The church is typical of rural churches, homemade and grass-roofed, not bad, but not great.

Mulongo wants me to meet the schoolmaster in this village. He's an enthusiastic young man I take an instant liking to. Here is one of the Congo's best and brightest. He has been appointed here by the bishop, right out of university.

He shows us around the school, highlighting the buildings he is proud of and acknowledging the ones that are sad, and he's right in both cases. Mulongo is also both proud and sad. This young man is his pride and joy, the best of his district team, but this school is typical of the challenge. There is just not enough funding, here or anywhere in the district.

I see two things: One, the leadership needed is here and in place. Two, these leaders are sent without support to do the impossible and will soon burn out and either move back to the city to find salaries worthy of their education or condemn themselves to lives of poverty, failure, and despair.

This point is important enough to repeat it for emphasis: The leadership needed in the Congo is here, in place, and ready to do the hard work, even in the most remote districts. Indeed, they are already doing the hard work, and they are exhausted. They are unpaid and unsupported. They are burning out. In many cases, they are, quite literally, dying.

This young schoolteacher in a village 30 kilometers outside of Mulongo is typical of the young adults coming out of the university now filled with hope and eager to get to the work. If I were a typical American on a mission-tourist trip, this is the young man I'd go back to the States and tell all my friends about in order to raise tons of money to build his school. But I'm going to meet twenty more just like him. My job isn't to fix his school; it's to figure out how we can create a system in which he thrives, a system in which his work is rewarded.

It is another 30 or so kilometers to the village of Mulongo, and in that time it begins to rain steadily, but not hard. I decide to put on my gray pullover raincoat that rolls up into its own carrying sack. It's a jacket that I've had for years, even though I don't normally like to put on rain gear because the plastic makes me sticky and I'd rather just get wet. Someday, I'd like to invest serious money in a rain jacket that breathes, but today is a perfect time to put on my cheap one: the temperature is cold enough, and the rain is steady enough.

The road is turning from sand to rocks. The land falls to our left and rises to our right, where grass-roofed houses are built on rocky formations and goats climb among them. On our left we begin to see glimpses of Lake Kabamba. The village of Mulongo can't be far now, but Lake Kabamba is big enough to have its own horizon, and the road gets worse with its large rocks. We ride another 3 kilometers downhill on these rocks, then another 3 or 4 kilometers uphill—not too steep, but the rocks make it technical.

Finally, the scouts appear. The ride is over. We are entering Mulongo.

# The Grand Well Come

*I* still have no idea what the *telos,* the end purpose, of this journey is to be, but arriving in Mulongo is clearly what Joseph Mulongo had planned.

At a concrete bridge, the road turns from country rocky trace to village street. Just on the other side of the bridge, a crowd of thousands has turned out to greet us— mostly youth and children, organized in troops of a hundred or so. Two young men are holding up a giant white bedsheet banner that bids us "well come" to the Mulongo Ecclesiastical District of *L'Eglise Methodiste-Unie,* a mix of French and English unified in blue letters. Along the sides of the street, teachers stand proudly with their schoolchildren holding banners for their schools, and social associations are present with their banners, too. Street children are running around underfoot, sometimes fascinated by our presence, but most of the time playing their own games in and around the trees. Young scouts are trying to police the children, to little avail. Even the switches they swat at them with have no sting and are ignored.

A man with a handheld bullhorn tries to organize the greeting, but each school is singing its own song, and his effort just annoys them. In the midst of this chaos of people and noise, the sea of children parts to make space for the official delegation. Three little girls with flowers step forward. One of them, I think, is Claudia, Mulongo's eldest daughter, who recites the greeting in English, but her voice is small and uncertain and can't compete with the crowd noise. A curtsy, and we're handed the flowers. This is just like the greeting at Kyubo, but ten times bigger. The district lay leader offers a couple of doves, one for me and one for Mulongo, complete with a speech about the doves representing peace.

The formalities complete, we break into hugs. I know that I should know many of these pastors and lay leaders. They know me. They're thrilled that we've arrived, and I'm thrilled that the journey has come to this destination. As far as the village of Mulongo is concerned, the whole purpose of this trip has been for Joseph Mulongo to bring me here. The new missionary has arrived.

We walk the long boulevard through the village in a parade, the children underfoot. A little urchin insists on walking right in front of me so that I occasionally step on the back of his flip-flop. I make a game of it and delight in my ability to remove his flip-flop without kicking him in the heel. A scout yells at him, and the boy disappears for a moment but is back as soon as he can squeeze through the crowd.

The boulevard is what's left over from colonial days. The giant eucalyptus trees, the trees of Mulongo's grandfather's story, are here, but the surface of the road is dirt and mud and holes now. We walk around several concrete bridges that are no longer serving their original function because years of rains have washed the road away from them. They are monuments to a glory day past, a day that profited only Europeans, who are no longer here to care about their bridges.

Mulongo is a large village. It claims to be the largest village in the Congo with between 60,000 and 100,000 people. It may well be. It doesn't have the total colonial package that towns like Kamina and Manono, and even Bunkeya, had. There's not much of an old European commercial downtown. The biggest colonial-era building is the original British Brethren missionary's impressive two-story house, which is falling down around its present poor occupants. In reality, Mulongo is a fishing village with a hospital. People come from hundreds of miles around to the Garenganze Hospital, a mission hospital run by the British Brethren. If you want to go back in time to see Dr. Albert Schweitzer's hospital, this is it.

Our parade ends at Centre United Methodist Church, the flagship church of the Mulongo District. Most district flagship congregations are housed in grand, old, tired, and well-worn structures built by missionaries two or three generations ago, but this one looks more like a storage depot with a shed roof that is about to fall off. The welcoming worship, however, is full of great music and dancing. The choirs are dressed in colorful uniforms, not hand-me-down robes from a church in America, but handmade, locally created works of art. The room is packed full of people, even on a weekday. I am intrigued.

Our bicycles have disappeared, and this is a piece of the trust walk I'm learning. When we entered the village, my bicycle with everything that I own was taken away from me by a young man whom I do not know. My laptop, clothes, and camping gear vanished into the village. I am mostly sure that this is not a problem, but there is a difference between believing something and trusting someone. The personal spiritual development aspect of this journey is the peace I'm finding in letting go of everything, every possession and every need. I'm thousands of miles away from home and hundreds of miles away from someone who speaks my language. I am totally dependent upon local hospitality, and I have no idea where I'll be staying while I'm in Mulongo. When a motorcycle appears to take me to the doctor's house, I jump on the back and we race away down streets and alleys, along fencerows, dodging sandpits, goats, and children. It's Mr. Toad's Wild Ride.

We pull up to a gated compound. The back side of the house faces the street and forms most of the street side of the compound wall. A large green water tank collects rain runoff from the roof. Solar panels cover the south side of the roof, and moss the north side. A tractor in the yard is missing so many major components that it is permanent yard art.

This is Dr. Serge's house, and I'll be staying here. Actually, this is the house of the director of the British Brethren Hospital, a post that Serge now holds. It was originally built for one of the missionary doctors here. It is postcolonial, but definitely missionary.

Standing together on the landing that leads to the French doors of the house's entry are Mimi and Mary, who are married to Serge and Mulongo, respectively. They are dressed in full-length, colorful African outfits, ready to head out to a party elsewhere in the village after they give me a friendly welcome. I can't imagine a high society life in the village, but apparently there is one, even if it is hidden from me. So far, this bicycle tour has shown me much poverty and misery, but that is not the whole picture of Congolese village life.

Mimi is from Lubumbashi, a city girl from a wealthy family. She's classy, funny, and clearly quite savvy. Mimi and Serge have only one child, Ariana. They are talking about having another, but two is their limit.

Mary is a curious mix of traditional and progressive, and her imagination about what life can be beyond the village has been stretched. She has family in Tanzania, and has spent time there learning some English and taking a course in computers. Mary has also graduated from the nursing school in Mulongo as an example to other women that they can be successful in what is generally a men's profession in the Congo. She has emerged as a leader in a world where only men are to be leaders. At the same time, Mary is a traditional wife and mother. When he and Mary got married, Mulongo said that he wanted only two children. Mary said she wanted five. Mulongo jokes that they compromised and had seven. A set of twins helps run up the count.

I have the bedroom at the end of the hall, the bachelor pad. Serge says that this was his room when he first came here unmarried. There were all kinds of village rumors about his lack of a wife and family. Children and adults alike stood brazenly outside the window that faces the street, watching for any action in his bedroom. With me, there's nothing to see, although I am aware that people are watching.

My panniers are delivered and I unload them. The dry clothing goes in the wardrobe along with medicines and toiletries. The wet, stinky clothes are laid out on the floor to dry. I'll wash them in the bathtub when it's my turn. I ask about my bicycle and am informed that Éléphant has taken it to clean and oil it. I'll get it back tomorrow or whenever.

Shabana and Prospère are in the other guest room. Éléphant and Mulongo have gone home to their families. I'm told that there is a *mzungu*-grade guesthouse here for the British Brethren missionary doctors who come seasonally. We're not staying there because they don't allow Congolese, and Mulongo understands that I don't want to be that kind of missionary.

The British Brethren missionaries set me off with their neo-apartheid attitudes. Jeff Hoover tells me they are not a church or a denomination, but a Bible-study movement in the British Isles and throughout the Commonwealth. They have a mission society that has been sending missionaries to the Congo from Ireland, Australia, and New Zealand for nearly 100 years. Here they are called *Garenganze,* after a river where the first British Brethren missionary set up a mission station. (Methodists were originally called *Springerites,* after the first Methodist missionary, but the name didn't stick.) In the Congo, at least around here, the Garenganze is a church with preachers and congregations, and they are known as conservative in a colonialist way.

Mulongo and I pass a Garenganze church while walking through the village one day, and he remarks on how their conservatism was costing them the youth. The Garenganze sing only hymns brought by the missionaries, denying the youth choirs guitars, electronic keyboards, and the free expression of creating new hymns. On top of that, despite good biblical scholarship, their sermons are long, dry, and preachy.

The funny thing about Mulongo's remark that the Congolese consider the Garenganze too conservative is that the General Conference of The United Methodist Church considers the Congolese delegates as the conservatives. While this may be so in the General Conference setting, the United Methodists in Mulongo are considered to be the progressive church. When I think about it, that is also true in Indiana. Indiana is considered a conservative conference among United Methodists nationwide, but I had a colleague pastor tell me that the church he was serving might look conservative to the rest of the conference, but in its community, it is seen as the liberal church. I guess it's all relative.

Back in 1996, my wife, Teri, and I were invited to a wedding in the village of Kasaji to be held in a Garenganze church. We joined the party as friends of the groom, a widowed United Methodist pastor, and this has been the only wedding I've ever attended where the groom made a bigger entrance than the bride, a widow who was a member of the Garenganze congregation. The bride came in first, and her entrance was so subdued that I missed it. When did that happen? The groom, on the other hand, came in with a loud posse of friends who carried him down the aisle. There was so much hootin' and hollerin' that when the pastor stepped forward to begin the ceremony, we Methodists were scolded for our lack of appropriate churchly decorum, and I've never been so proud to be a Methodist, not since

Scout begged Atticus to play for the Methodists in the softball game at the summer picnic.

This wedding was also the first time that I saw a Congolese pastor translating for another Congolese pastor, my introduction to the fact that in any given community, there may be multiple languages among the people.

Following the big community feast after the wedding ceremony, Teri and I were invited to the home of the British Brethren missionary doctor for tea. Ntambo escorted us there but was not invited into the home, a detail I missed but Teri noted. We were served a proper tea and offered a strange bit of hospitality: If we needed it, we could use their bathroom for bathing, and the language was blatantly racist. I guess they thought we weren't being cared for in a white people way by our black hosts. When I asked our elderly host about his replacement, he was critical of the Congolese doctor who was already on-site to replace him, and his racism wasn't even subtle. I thought, *How is it you can spend your whole life in service to Africans and have this much contempt for them?* I could only hope that this doctor was the last of his generation. When Ntambo came to pick us up, he waited outside. This I will never forget: The man who was not welcomed into the home of a missionary became a bishop.

As I settle into Serge's home, Mulongo disappears into the community. For days I don't see him. He's a busy man and he has been away too long, and he has come home to find too much work to catch up, too many projects to be coordinated. Meanwhile, Shabana has been drafted to teach medical English at the nursing school. When Prospère receives word that his wife in Kamina has given birth to twins, we send him with our blessings off to his family, although he promises to rejoin us on the road as soon as he can. Éléphant is busy with his fishing and his mechanics. We're going to be in Mulongo for two weeks, and I'm left alone to rest for now.

Books being too heavy to carry on a bicycle, I bought a Nook before leaving Indiana and loaded it with a Bible, some French lessons, a bicycle maintenance manual, two ancient biographies of David Livingstone from university libraries, and for the long read, Walter Isaacson's biography of Steve Jobs.

There is a TV in Serge's living room, which reminds me a little of home, but there are no broadcast or satellite channels. They have a home movie video of the family vacation to Kinshasa, including an amusement park. Then there are the videos of Christian singers, mostly made in Tanzania, and, of all things, an episode of *24* in French. Ah, Jack Bauer speaking French. Serge seldom turned on the TV, and then it required starting up the generator that sat outside in the *paillotte,* the outdoor pavilion. I read a lot on the road.

There is no community power grid, and the solar panels on the roof provide just enough power to recharge cell phones. Laptops drain the power quickly, so the limit to how many computers can be charged at a time is one. My Nook falls somewhere between a phone and a laptop. Generator time in the evening is used to get everything charged.

Mulongo hasn't taken me out on pastoral calls yet, which is unusual for our village visits. I think that he is not immune to the tendency to hide his reality from outsiders. Perhaps he is concerned about how I would rate his work if I saw him in action as a pastor. The truth is that I am impressed with the quality of his work. He embodies the key tenet of pastoral care: Show up and pray with.

One day, Mulongo and I are walking through the village on our way to do some important thing that I've since forgotten. He apologizes to me for stopping at a house on our way, saying, "They have lost their mother. I need to stop and say, 'Thank you.'" As he goes into the yard to greet the mourning family, I stand there thinking, *What a peculiar way to put it: They have lost a loved one, and I need to stop and say "Thank you."*

Mulongo had, of course, said this to me in English, which he speaks very well, but occasionally his other languages slip into his speaking. I realize that the Kiluba word for *thank you* (*wafwako*) is also the word for *I'm sorry.* It is a multipurpose word that varies in its meaning by inflection. That being said, what a wonderful way to greet a mourning friend: "Thank you."

## Kamina, 1997

*B*ack in 1997, Bishop Ntambo called me up to Kamina from Likasi for an orientation to the conference. In the past, all such orientation had been done missionary to missionary, but the bishop had organized a new program in which Congolese conference leaders would orient the new missionaries, not other missionaries. Radical. The first missionary to receive this orientation was a young agriculturalist from France, whom I met once over a platter of pan-fried grubs, a delicacy for both Congolese and French. Not to be shown up by a Frenchman, I ate my share (but no more than my share). I was the second missionary to receive this orientation. Nyembo Kikundulu, my #2 at Likasi, traveled with me to the orientation in Kamina by train. As a white guy, I could not travel alone with zero language skills and no experience traveling up-country in the Congo, even if the train was more reliable in those prewar days.

I learned a lot at the orientation. There were six instructors, each with a particular lesson to teach me, but all of them were present for every class. A six-to-one teacher-to-student ratio is powerful. Three lessons have stuck with me: one about culture, one about vocation, and one about identity.

The lesson about culture came at the bishop's table where we, all of us, had lunch every day. Our well-set table featured a traditional Luba meal of chicken, goat, fish, greens, palm sauce, and peanuts anchored with large mounds of *bukari*. Wanting me to eat as everyone does here, the bishop did not ask for *mzungu* alternatives as other hosts typically do. There was a generous amount of food on the table, and we ate communally with our hands, not with silverware.

The oddest thing about these meals for me was that my companions were all men. Although the team of instructors included at least one woman, we were dining at the Congolese men's table in its traditional form. It bothered me that the senior woman serving came out from the kitchen to invite us to the table and was asked by the bishop to say grace, after which she returned to the kitchen. I have a problem with someone saying grace over my food, then not being invited to sit down to the meal with me. After we had eaten, the remaining food would go back to the kitchen, where the women who had prepared it and blessed it would eat. When the women in the kitchen were finished eating, the food then went to the children in the yard. There was no concept of a family table.

On the third day, in the middle of lunch, Nyembo spoke up: "This is why our children are dying."

This had to be the bravest, bluntest, harshest criticism of the social order possible. At the bishop's table, Nyembo declared that the very order of life was killing the children—not malaria, not typhoid, not war, but the way they ordered their lives. You cannot imagine what an insult that was to the bishop who was trying to introduce me to the social life of the people I came to serve, and what a challenge it was to the church leadership, who were enjoying the benefits of this social order. They replicated this order in their own homes, which is where it becomes problematic. By the time what remains of the more modest everyday meal gets to their children, there is little left.

In standing up like this, Nyembo has presented the role of the pastor/preacher/theologian in community development. No amount of nutrition training or vaccinations or projects to drill wells or provide mosquito nets is going to have the power of a pastor who looks at the social order and declares, "This is why our children are dying!" Nyembo may or may not have the answer. He has, however, pushed the question beyond the normal, and ineffective, responses to the symptoms of malnutrition and disease. He has seen a system at work and its downstream result. Since this eventful meal, I have eaten in Nyembo's home many times. He and his wife, a nurse, have two children who eat their meals at the family table. Their children are bright-eyed and smart and full of life. I've seen too many children dull of eye and lifeless to not notice a difference.

Please don't read this and compare Congolese culture with American culture. Lord knows that our children are dying from the food we are feeding them and the way that we feed them. There is plenty of room for debate within a given society, Congolese or American. I was trained both in the officer's wardroom of a U.S. Navy ship, where we were served in much the same way as I was now being served at the bishop's table, and in the field as a U.S. Marine second lieutenant, where officers ate last, in reverse order of rank. The U.S. Marine Corps way seems to me to be more like the way of Jesus than the navy wardroom or bishop's table.

Nyembo's act of civil disobedience was a formative moment for me in 1997 as I was just beginning my work as a missionary. It helped me see that the pastor/theologian is the key to community development. I contend that the missionary evangelists missed the mark in messaging the Gospel. They preached a Gospel honed on the American frontier, which does not fit here. My contention is that the issues in the Congo now are more like the issues of first-century Galilee than of the American frontier, so we should return to the original generative themes that Jesus addressed, where we will find the issues that present-day Congolese people face.

The second lesson that has stuck with me from the 1997 orientation in Kamina is about vocation. One of the sessions focused on what kind of missionary I would be. We were all looking at each other around the circle. Being polite, each of my instructors tried hard not to make an open indictment of his or her least favorite missionary. Their dissatisfaction with the work and behavior of some missionaries was evident, however. One elder cut to the quick. Pointing his bony finger at me, he said firmly, "You're a pastor. Be a pastor."

That stuck.

All of the messages I was receiving from the institutional church, including the missionary training I had received in Atlanta, was that I was leaving the profession of pastor to become a missionary. I recognize that there are plenty of missionaries who are not pastors. There are doctors, nurses, agriculturalists, architects, administrators, and on and on. But I'm a pastor. The fact that I'm not leading a congregation in Indiana does not make me not a pastor. The fact that I find myself in Africa with no clear job description does not make me not a pastor. Whatever I end up doing here, I'm a pastor. Be a pastor.

When I got back to Likasi, I started being a pastor. One of our women seminarians was married to a pastor in a fishing village on a lake not too far away. I made an appointment to spend a day shadowing him in his pastoral duties. After riding my bicycle two hours to his village, I followed him around through the market and from door to door as he mingled with the people and checked on his flock. When he received word that a baby had died, we went to the morgue and sat with the mother and her dead child. The morgue was a tiny brick building, kept cool by cave-like construction. The room was just large enough for a stone slab, table height, where the body was laid out. I've seen sobbing mothers and hysterical mothers, but this mother just sat there on a small stool in the corner, silent. The pastor prayed with her while I just stood next to the baby, praying. Have you ever stared at a lifeless baby until you almost believed that his little chest had moved?

So, on the advice of an elder in the North Katanga Conference in Kamina, I was a pastor. From that day on, every community development puzzle that began with the question "Why are our children dying?" had to be married to a theological question to find an effective answer. Not only am I a pastor, but my task as a missionary is to walk alongside pastors.

The third lesson that has stayed with me from that orientation in Kamina also happened during lunch at the bishop's table, and it was about identity. I was bravely trying to work on my Swahili, and annoying everyone, I'm sure.

"*Bantu* means people," I said to Ntambo. "Are all people Bantu?"

"Most, but not all."

"Am I Bantu?"

"No. You are Tutsi."

That knocked me off the foundation I thought I had established with him. For the previous few years, I had considered Ntambo my best friend. Not my best African friend, not my best black friend, but my best friend. We had become friends before he became a bishop. In fact, it was the work that we had done together that helped make him a bishop. His success was my success. Even though he was now my bishop, I thought of him as my close friend. We walked the streets of Lubumbashi holding hands, a thing that Congolese men do when they are good friends. Now he tells me that I can never be Bantu. I will always be Tutsi. I will always be an outsider.

For Ntambo, who has spent time in Burundi, a Tutsi is viewed as smarter than a Bantu. When he rebuilt the conference offices after the war, Ntambo hired a Tutsi contractor to do the work. A Tutsi is trusted to do a better job, but a Tutsi is always an outsider, always the enemy. Like the message that I should be a pastor, the message that I would always be the outsider was strong and clear. I would be valued for my intelligence, but always an outsider.

As much as that hurt, it was, in a way, liberating. My role in the community was getting defined. I serve the community, but I will never be one of the community. I have become a person without a people. I don't fit in the church in America and I don't belong here.

On a macro level, however, this is a clue to the problem of poverty here. There is so little sense of self-worth and self-confidence that it is always assumed that an outsider (Tutsi or American) is better, smarter. Of course, I don't buy the assumption that Tutsis or Americans are smarter. One day a young Congolese man said to me, "The difference between Africans and Americans is that Americans are smarter." That kind of thinking is deadly.

# Kamina's Lessons in Mulongo

Staying in one village for two weeks means I have more energy for thinking, and the lessons from my orientation in Kamina in 1997 are with me in Mulongo in 2010. One of the contrasts between Congolese life and American life that is frequently pointed out by both missionaries and the Congolese themselves is the way these two cultures treat children. The often-stated belief is that children in the Congo are ignored. Children are potential adults, but until then, they are worth nothing. This is one of those racist ideas repeated so often by so many that it becomes a truism. The defense goes that Congolese must have lots of children because infant mortality is so high, and one's children are the only pension plan, the only hope of support in old age. Some children will die, some will move away, some will turn out to be worthless. Have many. I have had Congolese leaders tell me this, even though my observation is that, even though it has some truth in practice, this is not really how they feel about their children. I suspect that this is a case of telling me what they think that I believe about them.

This is an area that invites much more sitting and listening and observing. The issue of childhood in the Congo illustrates one of the arguments of this book: We are crafting community development programs at the shallow end of our understanding of a culture.

The traditional men's table with the women eating in the kitchen and the children later feeds the idea that children are undervalued in the Congo. Serge and Mimi are like Nyembo and his wife, what might be considered here as more *mzungu*. Nyembo's and Serge's households interact with their children in a more Western way. I'm trying not to place a value judgement on this difference, but rather mark the apparent change for reflection. Serge and Mimi are a part of an emerging middle class of university-trained professionals. Their financial security is in their education, not their children. In fact, for them, the model is turned upside down. Children are now an expense. The decision becomes whether to spread the wealth over several children or concentrate it on one or two. When you come into Serge and Mimi's house, you see a front room filled with baby furniture and toys. Ariana is undoubtedly the most spoiled child in all of the Congo, and Serge is trying to assemble the toys and furniture without instructions.

Meanwhile, Serge is also the Albert Schweitzer of Mulongo. First, his hospital is no better equipped than Schweitzer's was fifty years ago. Second, even though Serge is Congolese, trained in Lubumbashi, it is at great personal sacrifice and professional risk that he has come here to be the village doctor instead of staying in Lubumbashi on the staff of a hospital there. This decision was part career strategy—to build experience faster than he might in a large staff hospital in the city—but it was also sacrificial. In the village, Serge has become both surgeon and internist. He does surgery three days a week: Mondays, Wednesdays, and Fridays. On Tuesdays and Thursdays, he does rounds. At night, he is on his laptop studying new procedures. Every morning, regardless of the day, there are people waiting at his gate, and he treats them with generous kindness and patience. He believes in and truly enjoys what he is doing. I am a huge fan of Dr. Serge.

It is because I have met doctors like Serge that I am so critical of medical mission initiatives coming out of the United States, especially the parachute-drop-style ones. I often come across as Mr. Negative about Everything Apple Pie, but the overhead and executive salaries of those programs could help so many doctors like Serge who need just a little boost to support their work.

On the subjects of stereotypes, Serge's hospital, and the call to be a pastor, Joseph Mulongo has the problem of being the district superintendent in a district that has a good hospital. The bishop, in his care for his pastors, appoints those who need to be close to a hospital to the Mulongo District exactly because it has a hospital. Therefore, the Mulongo District has way more than its share of sick and dying pastors. Joseph Mulongo has become the pastor to a lot of sick pastors and a supervisor of a district that is understaffed because his pastors are more sick than healthy.

Mulongo and I go to the hospital to visit a pastor whose legs Serge had just amputated because of complications with diabetes. People will tell you that suicide is a concept unknown to the Congolese, that it is unthinkable. And yet, we sit and pray with a pastor who wants to end his life because it is over, and he doesn't want to be a bother to his children. It is his adult children who are begging Mulongo to talk their father out of suicide. People are never only what cultural stereotypes say they are. Deep down, when we take the time to listen, we are all the same, and we are each different.

# Church Visits Around Mulongo

*A*fter a few days' rest, we start to make church visits in and around Mulongo. Éléphant had brought back my bicycle, all clean and oiled, like new. I put on one rear pannier for incidentals I might need for a day trip. We get out on the road on unloaded bicycles that feel so light. If it weren't for the sand, we would be riding fast. It takes me two starts to get going, burying the front wheel in the sand on the first attempt of the morning. Sand is a common problem in the villages, where the streets and alleys are filled with sand traps, even in the wet season.

It is the wet season and the creeks are up. As we're approaching the northern edge of the village, we are stopped by a creek that has jumped out of its banks. The bridge is broken, but there are half a dozen young men there to direct us and help us navigate the workaround. This is the norm. The bridge doesn't get fixed, but a creative way to live without it is invented. A whole new service industry springs up around the problem as young entrepreneurs find a place for their otherwise unemployed energy. My bike is carried through the swollen creek by someone who knows where the rocks are as I do my best high-wire act across the makeshift log walkway. This is so common that I'll end up doing it hundreds of times over hundreds of rivers and creeks.

I ask Mulongo if we should pay the young men for their help. He shakes his head no. I'm certain that there is an economic system at work here, but I don't understand it. I don't know how the village exchanges goods and services in these informal transactions. I do know, however, that I don't want to upstage Mulongo, and undermine his community leadership, by pulling out money. The truth is that I don't carry money because Mulongo handles all financial transactions. I give Mulongo my $100 bills, and he changes them into Congolese francs as needed. If I wanted to buy a young man a Coke, I'd have to ask Mulongo for the 500 francs.

The church we are visiting today is on the edge of the village. It was damaged, nearly destroyed, by the monsoon-like rains that brought severe flooding, destruction of homes and churches, and an epidemic of cholera to the village of Mulongo and much of Katanga last year. The north wall of the church is completely collapsed. The remaining walls are at about half height. There is a temporary stick-and-grass roof that gives the church its shape. We lean our bikes against the ruins of the walls, duck our heads, and walk "inside." There are a couple of log benches on the dirt floor. We are invited to sit. The pastor goes through his pitch, the story of the church's falling and the appeal for help to rebuild it.

We are going to see a hundred like this one. Three today. What the war didn't destroy, the floods did.

The day's tour of churches ends back in Mulongo at a church that once had been pastored by the missionary Ken Vance, although the congregation has built a new building since his time. Now the new building has become too small for the growing congregation and an even newer building is being built. The new-new walls are being built around the existing, actively used building, like a courtyard around the church. Eventually, the outer church will have a roof and the inner church will be taken down. That's the plan, anyway. I've seen it done in other places, even sometimes successfully.

We are treated to a worship service there. Truthfully, I don't like it much. This church, like many churches, is now copying Christian contemporary as the new model for evangelism. I'm constantly asked by choirs and music directors to help them buy keyboards. I never do. I've even been asked to buy those handheld megaphone horn things—what do you call them? Bullhorns. They're wanted for evangelism. I can't imagine anything more unlike good news than the annoying crackle of a bullhorn turned up full volume shouting "Jesus" at me. Traditional Bantu worship with drums and singing and dancing is a disappearing experience. One of the reasons I'm going deeper into the remote districts is to run away from electricity and sit on a dirt floor, under a grass roof, and appreciate the raw drums and dancing. Primitive is not a pejorative. Oh well, to each his own.

This is where I have to check my own prejudices and preferences. I can't let my love for the old ways to stand in the way of progress. I shouldn't stifle the enthusiasm of a new generation and a desire for electric instruments. I'm just not going to pay for it. However, I'm mild in my love for the old and dislike of the new. Bishop Ntambo is outspoken on the subject. If there aren't traditional drums, it's not worship. If I even suggest that I appreciate one of these modern worship services, he sneers. And I have appreciated some of these modern services. The first time I saw a homemade electric guitar, powered by a 12-volt battery borrowed from a car, I was blown away. I learned that day that the poverty here is not the result of lack of intelligence. One Sunday my young friends took me to the chapel at the University of Lubumbashi. The choir and musicians there led us in an opening prayer that went on for twenty minutes with more movements than a symphony. I was transported to the Third Heaven, where I swear I heard Stevie Nicks. It was a fusion of hymn, power rock, classical, and traditional African. Forget gold, diamonds, and coltan—the wealth of the Congo is the talent, the brilliance, of its youth.

The worship service at Ken Vance's old church is not brilliant, creative, or inspired. Nor is it inspiring. The music director is his own one-man show, full of himself and his electronic keyboard. The keyboard is powered by a generator, the getting started of which is a huge distraction, as God is being asked to wait in the wings until this lousy generator can be hooked up and running. The worst, though, is the worship leader's use of the American pop tunes that had been preloaded onto the keyboard. He samples these tunes at the most inappropriate times in the service. I see T-shirts with inappropriate messages on them worn in worship all the time, and I just smile to myself, but the canned American pop tunes on an electronic keyboard cross the line for me. Just because I have disciplined myself to not get involved in these kinds of local church worship discussions doesn't mean that I have to like what I see and hear. Give me drums, please. Also, I wonder what the pastor thinks of this worship leader. My bet is that they don't get along. I'll bet that this worship leader is the pastor's worst nightmare. I wonder what Ken Vance would think.

I keep running into the tracks that other missionaries have left behind, and I feel the need to write about them, even though I did not intend to write a book about the missionaries I have known, and especially because I did intend to write a book criticizing the missiology of the church for which these missionaries worked.

I first met Ken Vance in 1991 when I was in the Congo with a group from Indiana, and he was one of the three missionary pilots who were ferrying us around. We bonded over being aviators. Ken was the only one of our pilots who wore a pilot's uniform shirt with the wings pinned over the pocket. As a former naval aviator and U.S. Marine Corps helicopter pilot, that's what I would have chosen to wear when flying a plane, too.

Several years later, Ken and his wife, Deb, were back in Indiana for an operation on one of their children, and I found a like mind in Ken as I was struggling with my call to come to the Congo as a missionary. When we visited in the hallway of that hospital in Indianapolis, I found that we were on the same page, reading from the same book, with our understandings of ministry. Ken told me that he couldn't ever come back to Indiana as a pastor. The stakes were too low, the issues too trivial.

After the violence of 1991 and the resulting missionary evacuation, when Ken and Deb did return to the Congo, he went back as a pastor, not a pilot. The bishop appointed him to Mulongo. I remember at the time trying to imagine what it would be like to move my family to an up-country village without electricity and survive. In fact, it didn't go well for them, survival-wise. Deb was bitten by a black mamba that their pet cat had brought into the house. With no refrigeration, there was no antivenom on hand. Deb did survive the bite but was at death's door for several days. Ken and Deb were the last resident missionaries in Mulongo. If I were to stay in Mulongo as the missionary, I would be pleased to be seen as a continuation of their ministry.

# The Nursing School

One of my assignments on this expedition is to check out the nursing school in Mulongo. Back in 2008 I had received a phone call from Denver Thornton, a lawyer in Arkansas, a Bill Clintonesque good old boy, who had been recruited to invest in a nursing school in Mulongo by Dr. Ivan Mulongo. (Yes, I know that there are many Mulongos in this story.) Denver was taken in by Ivan's story but still a bit cautious, and he wanted some proof of the efficacy of this nursing school, or even of its existence. He wanted someone on the ground to verify it. He wanted me to go to Mulongo and report back to him.

Why me? Long story. Denver and his wife, Robin, who is the one who really is into missions, gave a substantial amount of money to do a well project in Kamina and felt as if they had been ripped off. At the very least, they couldn't get any feedback on their wells. (I'll go to Kamina next year and check on his wells. In the meantime, I'll try to talk another donor down from trying to micromanage their mission giving in the field.) Somehow, as Denver was calling everybody in The United Methodist Church about his frustration, he was given my daughter Taylor's name by a General Board of Global Ministries (GBGM) staffer in New York. He called her and now believes that she is the only one who has told him the straight truth about what is going on in the Congo. Taylor told him to call me, as I would be riding through Mulongo. At this point, I didn't know Denver any more than I knew the nursing school in Mulongo. He may very well turn out to be a nut case. Lord knows that I've known my share. In my years of inner-city ministry experience, I've had to deal with too many crazy donors whose dreams turned out to be my nightmares.

Now that I'm here in Mulongo, I need to find out about this nursing school. The history of the school relates to the recent war. Dr. Serge's predecessor, Dr. Ivan Mulongo, also a United Methodist, was the chief of the British Brethren hospital in Mulongo during the war when there was a shortage of nurses and no way to train them. Many were given fewer than six weeks of training and sent into the field to do their damage. Dr. Ivan determined to reverse this medical disaster. He created a three-year, fully accredited nursing school.

Housing the nursing school has been a challenge. At first Dr. Ivan ran his United Methodist nursing school out of the British Brethren Hospital, and for four years, the school operated in rented and borrowed facilities. The Ministry of Education, however, requires all university-level schools to have their own campuses in order to maintain accreditation, so the nursing school needed to build a building. The local chief had given them the land, and bricks had been made and fired. They now needed to raise the money for cement, timbers, and roofing (and doors and windows, etc., etc.). Dr. Ivan has since been elected to Parliament and spends most of his time in Kinshasa. Dr. Serge has replaced him at the hospital and as the director of the nursing school, and Joseph Mulongo chairs the nursing school board.

We take a day to visit the nursing school in its rented classroom. Shabana is busy teaching medical English to the students. Medical English is a required course, and although it doesn't make nurses fluent in English, it does make them capable of reading drug labels. Many of the students have been awaiting this class in order to graduate. Shabana has been a godsend for them, and it may be that the only purpose for our ride was to get these students their medical English class. We can't leave until finals are graded, and Shabana's teaching stretches our two weeks in Mulongo into three.

Under the unbearably hot afternoon sun, we take the long walk up the hill to see the building site. The Grand Chief has given the nursing school a prime piece of land with an incredible view overlooking Lake Kabamba. The ground is nothing but rocks and sand and scrub brush. There's a ditch line dug for the foundation and a pile of rocks around, but that's pretty much it. The nursing school building isn't much beyond the dream phase.

I have to make a decision here. Does Friendly Planet Missiology get behind this project? If we do, and it fails, as 99 percent of the projects I've seen so far have, then FPM is finished. Overstated? I don't think so. I've been shown a lot of projects and have been asked to help. I'll see a lot more before this trip is over. It's my call now. This is the one we're going to put our name on. Go big, or go home.

Actually, we're not picking a project. We're picking a team. Ivan (whom I've yet to meet), Joseph Mulongo, Mary Kabanga, Dr. Serge, Denver, and Robin—this is our team. We really don't pick them. They are given to us. Taylor calls this *theostitious,* which applies not to things that we have done ourselves, but to moments when we recognize that God—or the universe, or however you understand God or the universe—moves for good. The only talent I can claim is the talent to see God at work, or the universe turning, or God turning the universe. Even so, there have been many times when I've gotten it wrong, and some times that maybe I got it right but everyone else got it wrong. Like children on the playground, we pick Ivan, Joseph, Mary, Serge, Denver, and Robin. Now to tell Denver that it'll take $15,000 to get this project started.

We're on a roll. The next day a delegation of female nursing school students show up at the house. Unlike in America, where most nurses are women, in the Congo most nurses are men and the female nurse is the exception. There is a grassroots movement to change that in the Mulongo District as women in the villages demand that they be served by female nurses, not men. There may be an outside Western cultural influence, but if there is, it's reinforcing an empowerment that women are claiming.

There is resistance to this change, though. The village nurse occupies a place of authority and honor in the community, and the unscrupulous can leverage this important position for income. Men, in general, are not willingly letting women into the profession. Some men, however, like Serge and Mulongo, see the importance of this social change. They are backing the women who want to be nurses because it is the right thing for these women as well as a good thing for the community, especially the women and children.

Mary Kabanga, Joseph Mulongo's wife, was in the first class of female nurses at Dr. Ivan's United Methodist nursing school. She enrolled not only for herself, but also to encourage others to join her in becoming a nurse. When Mulongo supported his wife in her schooling, other men asked him why he was allowing his wife to become a prostitute. Corruption is the norm in higher education in the Congo. While men pay bribes, women are expected to give their professors sex in return for good grades. Thus, if a woman is succeeding at school, she must be a prostitute. In addition to a commitment to equal education for women, United Methodist universities are building a reputation for quality instruction by professors who are not corrupt. They don't take bribes and they don't rape their female students.

The delegation of female nursing school students meet with me in the *paillotte* in the yard. They bring gifts: a live rabbit, which we eat later that week, and a carved walking stick, which stands next to my fireplace in Indiana. The women state their goals. First, they want the student body of the nursing school to be half women. Second, they want the nursing staff of the hospital to be half women.

I love it when we can get behind a movement like this. It's one thing to come into a community and try to tell people what they need to do to change their lives. It's an entirely other level when the movement is already moving and we get to give it just a little push. Even if we can't provide the money needed, just listening and agreeing gives power to the movement.

## Village Listening Sessions

*W*hile I'm in Mulongo, I continue to refine my listening sessions. I do a full-blown leadership development session with district leaders and pastors at the Centre United Methodist Church, but I'm not happy with the presentation yet. It's still too "talking head" for me, but I'm getting better with each attempt. Mulongo translates for me and is internalizing the pitch. It won't be long before I can disappear and he will take over. He is giving me courage. His enthusiasm in translating and explaining the ideas tells me that I'm on the right track.

When we ride out to a small village church for one of our deep listening sessions, we find the whole village gathered in the tiny grass-roofed church. We are playing to packed houses. I open with the short version of our stump speech. "I know of your poverty, but you are rich!" (Rev. 2:9) I tell them that everything we need, God has already provided. That feels harsh every time I say it to a group of people suffering in this poverty, but somehow, it works. It sets the attitude for the meeting. People know that as they present their problems, they have to shape their appeal in a way that leverages their own strengths. They seem honored to be able to present their ideas, rather than resort to begging.

If it takes a village to raise a child, I'd like to see a research paper written on what kind of different people it takes to make a village. It seems that there is a pattern. In the next three years, we're going to do a hundred of these sessions, at least. We'll do so many that I'll understand what is being said, even if it is in French, Swahili, or Kiluba. I'll be able to look out into the audience and pick out who is going to speak and which issue he or she is going to present. It's funny. Every village has exactly the same people. The same faces are in the choir. Exactly the same people are in leadership. Exactly the same people show up at these meetings. They sit in exactly the same places.

In this meeting, as in each and every one of them, we heard the chief speak first. There are chiefs who have grand homes and are wealthy beyond the ordinary villager. Then there are chiefs who are as poor as the villagers they lead. This chief is one of the latter, and I am impressed with his wisdom. He is able to articulate the problems of the village and even make a pretty good case for his plan to turn this poverty into progress.

Mulongo manages the meeting, making certain that there is a balance between respecting the social order and making it possible for all voices to get heard. A young adult woman, maybe in her 30s and well-dressed for this poor village, stands up in the back to speak. She is poised and articulate.

"When I was a child, my parents didn't send me to school. I can't read or write." Damn, my heart breaks, and tears well up. I can't stand the poignancy of seeing a young woman so poised, so attractive, so strong, break through the shame and announce to this strange visitor, "I can't read." But she isn't finished. She has a proposal: "We women grind grain all day by hand. This takes hours. If we had a mill, that would give us time to go to learn to read and write. We could have a school for women who didn't get to go to school as children." She is the leadership voice from the back row.

There is so much here to unpack. I'm going to hear time and time again how women's literacy is one of the top community concerns. It will come in consistently in the top three, alternating with safe drinking water and health care. Here in the Congo, I am awoken every morning at daybreak around 6:00, not by the light, but by the sudden change in temperature that comes with the sun. When I wake I hear the women already at work. Their work begins at four in the morning. It won't end until after midnight. Life takes all day. Over time it will dawn on me how the issues of women's literacy, access to safe water, and quality health care are related.

## Leaving Mulongo

*I*'ve settled into my little room in Dr. Serge's house quite comfortably. I think that I'd make a good monk, or even a hermit. This is ultimately the permanent inner conflict of my life. My greatest happiness is to be with Teri, whether at home in our 1915 Craftsman bungalow on Main Street in Plainfield or on the beach in Fort Myers. Just being with her is more than enough for me. My vocation, though, is to live as a lone monk on a wandering quest. Even when I have no idea where I am, I don't feel lost. Rather than searching for something, I'm walking through the world as an observer, a watcher. In general, I don't feel a need to report on what I see. The only reason I'm writing this book is that I feel the pressure of the real world to produce a work product. Maybe there will be a financial payoff, but I doubt it. Maybe it's a story that needs to be told. (Strike "maybe.")

Both Teri and I find this conflict impossible and an unsolvable puzzle. She hates the separation, but she refuses to join me. And yet I can see that if we were to become a missionary couple, the creative tension of this puzzle would be removed, and whatever is out there yet to be discovered would be left hidden. So we have arrived at a compromise that's not really a compromise as much as it's an acceptance of an impossible war between vocation and vacation.

Thus I make my monk-sized bed, with its hospital mattress and mosquito net, so far from Teri and home. I wash my clothes in a bucket and tidy my things. It's a simple life that allows for time to read and reflect. I'm not a cloistered monk, though; I'm a traveler, and three weeks is long enough in one place. It's time to get back on the road.

Shabana has finished grading the papers of the nursing school students in his medical English course. We can now leave town.

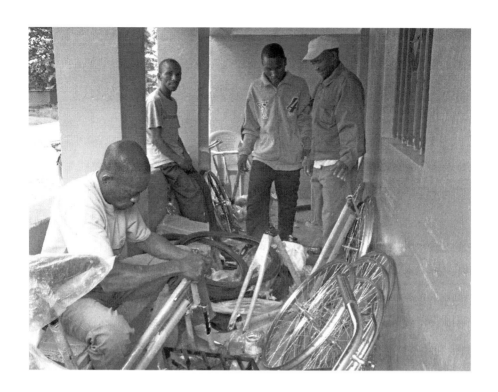

# Mulongo to Kabwe to Mwanza

*I*t feels good to be back on the bike again. Legs working. Moving. Physical exercise.

Dr. Serge is coming down with something, maybe just a cold. I've been feverish for a couple days. Conventional wisdom, common sense, might have suggested that I take a couple of days of bed rest to get over whatever my body is struggling with, but the cool wind of the morning in my face feels better than lying in bed with a fever.

Good-byes were exchanged last night in a traditional farewell party, complete with speeches and parting gifts. Each member of the team received a newly made shirt from the district. Because they were all made from the same bolt of cloth, we now have uniforms. The fact that we all received shirts indicates that all of us were valued for our visit. Shabana had been the surprise bonus. For the village of Mulongo, his teaching the medical English class at the nursing school alone was reason enough for our visit.

We're leaving without Prospère. We haven't heard from him in several days. I'm hoping that he'll rejoin us en route. Shabana received word that his uncle had died in Malemba. That's not too far out of our way, so he and Éléphant will break off for a quick detour to Malemba, to visit family and catch us on the other side of Mwanza. We'll split up at Kabwe.

We get up at 5:00 a.m. to make an early start. After an abbreviated breakfast, we are off. It's still dark, so we have our lights on. The bikes had been prepped the night before, and my bike feels strange fully loaded. We've been riding around the district for a couple of weeks with no baggage. The sand in the yard makes getting started a bit tricky. Mulongo leads us through the back alleys and shortcuts, many of which are filled with sand traps, but the first pirogue leaves the riverbank at first light, and Mulongo is determined to be on it. Always the pastor, though, he continues to greet folks as we depart. The greetings break his quick pace and give me a chance to catch up. We have to cross a couple of streams to get out of town, but by now we've crossed these before and know the secrets hiding under the water. It's trying to rain, just an early morning drizzle. With the stream crossings, the morning rain, and the dew on the tall grass, we're plenty wet. But we'll dry out as soon as the sun is up.

The road down to the river devolves into single track through the grasslands. In this season the grass is well over our heads. We're on and off our bikes as we negotiate the mud and water.

We're late. We missed the first boat. All that pushing and fast riding and now we wait for the next pirogue. Africa Time is not as simple and laid-back as you've been told, especially in the morning as the whole village is trying to push and shove to get a place on the first boat or first bus of the day. Miss a boat, or a bus, or a train, and you could be stuck until tomorrow, or the next day, or until Jesus comes. (When I reflect on Africa Time later, remind me to talk about Jesus Time.)

After the initial disappointment, we settle in to wait and find our place among the others waiting to cross the river. I take my cues from Mulongo, who is always the nonanxious presence in the crowd.

Finally, a pirogue arrives. It's large enough to hold our loaded bikes. I hang back out of the organized chaos of loading the boat. I have learned not to tell people how to do their jobs, even when they're handling my stuff. My new $2,000 Cannondale T1 touring bike was purchased with the knowledge that it would be packed into airline cases, thrown on the backs of trucks, stacked in railroad freight cars, and balanced in canoes.

When it's my time, I wade through the water and find my place in the boat. Considering that we're in an overloaded dugout canoe just inches from the waterline, the whole thing is remarkably stable. A young man in a red Manchester United T-shirt is standing in the bow with a long paddle, and his senior is standing in the stern with his paddle. They push off and we begin the half-hour crossing of two rivers and the marshlands between them.

While planning this expedition months ago, I had looked at this point on the map and asked, "Is there a bridge here?" The answer: "No." I could not imagine how one got a loaded bicycle across a river in a dugout canoe. But now a morning crossing feels routine. Anxiety level: 0. Zero.

On the other side, the bikes are off-loaded and we quickly get on the road. All business now. It's low river bottomland roads to Kabwe. Except for those occasional annoying patches of sand, the road's not too bad and we make good time. Feeling comfortable in the saddle. I'm aware of the slight fever, but I would rather be riding than resting. At Kabwe, Éléphant on the motorcycle and Shabana on his bicycle leave us for Malemba. Mulongo and I head up the mountain for Mwanza.

Not since the Mother of Mountains have we climbed like this. The rocky road zigzags its way up the mountain. We take the first shortcut between a zig and a zag. It is barely a footpath and so we get off and push. Straight up. Lifting our loaded bikes up over the short cliffs, rock climbing more than bikepacking. Too steep. Bad idea. We will pass on the next shortcut. This is hard work, and the dampness of my T-shirt from the morning rain is replaced by sweat from the heat and struggle. It's some kind of sickness in my head that enjoys such suffering. However, today the sickness in my head may be more body than soul.

On the steep mountain road to Mwanza, we run into the reason for the war: the coltan mines. They're no more than open pits, dug by hand by strong black men. The minerals just look like dirt. Some white mercenaries, I'm guessing South African, will drive through in a jungle tricked-out Land Rover and buy up all the coltan the men have dug. It could be opium in Afghanistan or cocaine in Columbia. In the Congo it's coltan. It's hard to get your head around the fact that more than six million Congolese have died for this mineral. It's harder to accept that people with cell phones and laptops in America don't know what's in their phones, where it came from, or how inhumane the process of mining it is.

I'm looking over the edge of the road into a deep, hand-dug hole in the ground, a hole that has supplied the essential mineral for the Communication Age and in the process has killed millions. But that's the history of the Congo.

Coltan is not the first natural resource to harm the Congolese people. In *King Leopold's Ghost*, Adam Hochschild follows all characters in Joseph Conrad's *Heart of Darkness* and finds that behind this work of fiction are real people who did these things. Ten million Congolese were killed in the harvest of raw rubber, the essential raw material that made the American and European auto industries possible. The United States participated in this exploitation despite activists like Mark Twain who spoke out against it. From ivory to gold to rubber to tin to copper to diamonds to cobalt to uranium, it has been a nonstop robbing of resources that have built Western civilization. The U-235 used to build the atomic bombs that were dropped on Hiroshima and Nagasaki came from the Congo. Western civilization. What does that mean?

A story goes that when Albert Schweitzer was asked by a young reporter, "Dr. Schweitzer, now that you've been in Africa, what do you think of European civilization?" Schweitzer replied, "I think it would be a very good idea."

Our so-called Western civilization has been built on the raw minerals stolen out from under the feet of a people who remain among the poorest in the world. We've done so through direct colonial exploitation, through the propping up of African strongmen, and most recently through turning a blind eye to a pan-African border war. The people who live in the villages of eastern Congo have been beaten down, dehumanized, slaughtered, and raped, creating a perpetual state of demoralization. Coltan is now the mineral of the day. We kill millions of people, rape women and girls, and burn villages for our coltan.

Last year, Bishop Ntambo had sent me to Kalemie, where I was received as the first missionary to visit since the war. Man, were they glad to see me! But I was a bit puzzled that as I was being greeted as the first missionary to visit since the war, I was being hosted by an older missionary couple. (It turned out that they were Pentecostal, so it should be qualified that I was the first United Methodist missionary to visit Kalemie since the war.) The missionaries' house was among half a dozen homes built for the Belgian managers of the large and once profitable textile mill in Kalemie. As the textile mill is no longer operating, the houses are rented out to American missionaries, or wealthy African businesspeople, or, during the war, invading generals. These houses sit on a ridge line and overlook the whole city and its harbor and rail station. The veranda of the guest room I enjoyed had a view that rivals any villa on the Riviera or bungalow in the Caribbean, but it is also the perfect vantage point from which a general could direct a war, and so they did.

Ralph, the Pentecostal missionary whose courage I still admire and whose generosity and hospitality I cannot repay, had many a dinner conversation with the general who lived next door, whether Rwandan, Congolese, or Ugandan. They all put the same spin on the war: They weren't engaged in the atrocities. That was the other side.

What's closer to the truth is that the slaughter, rape, and pillage below them were a convenient distraction. The generals engaged in just enough war directing to keep their smuggling business protected while they moved gold and coltan back into their home countries. Fortunes were made, and they didn't even have to win the war.

These Pentecostal missionaries, who had rebelled against their denominational mission board and stayed through the war, were fired by their board. I was envious and imagined what it might have been like if I had ignored the evacuation order from the General Board of Global Ministries (GBGM) and had stayed in the Mitwaba District.

Having confessed my envy and having sucked in all the war stories these brave missionaries shared with me, I could see a picture of the war maybe only I was seeing. I saw what John described in Revelation 6:5–6:

> When he opened the third seal, I heard the third living creature call out, "Come!" I looked, and there was a black horse! Its rider held a pair of scales in his hand, and I heard what seemed to be a voice in the midst of the four living creatures saying, "A quart of wheat for a day's pay, and three quarts of

barley for a day's pay, but do not damage the olive oil and the wine!" (NRSV)

John presents the picture of the suffering of the people in a war, while the rich continue to get richer, even profiting from the war.

# Africa Time

*T*his mountain just keeps getting steeper. It's all pushing now. I have my head down and am focused on Mulongo ahead of me, watching one Reebok move ahead of the other. *Those used to be my Reeboks,* I'm thinking. They had developed an annoying squeak, and when Mulongo borrowed them one day, I asked him if he liked them. He said he did, and now they are his.

The only relief from the heat and the sweat is the rare patch of shade. The brush is thin in the rocky soil, and trees are pitiful. My mind wanders as I keep pushing. May as well tell you about Africa Time.

When I first met Ntambo, he was always making jokes about Africa Time. "Americans keep time. Africans make time." It always came as an excuse for why he was late or why a scheduled event didn't start on time. I don't buy it.

I don't buy this cultural stereotype that paints a picture of Africans as laid-back and lazy or, putting a positive spin on it, as more in tune with nature and not rushed by modern life. In urban settings, the early morning road rage rivals any U.S. beltway traffic jam. Bus passengers yell at late passengers and at bus drivers to leave the late ones. Bus drivers yell at other bus drivers. I don't see the laid-back making time.

The village comes alive at four in the morning. Men are in the fields before daybreak. Women start cooking before the roosters crow and don't stop until it's too dark to clean pots. When we get to the river at daybreak, fishermen are already bringing in the first catch of the day. The people may be as poor as the dirt floors of their huts, but schoolchildren are bathed and dressed in uniforms and sent off to class where they sit in neat rows, attentive to the teacher who expects them to be on time with homework completed. My new catchphrase is "Life takes all day." I've said that before, but it needs repeating. Life takes all day, and then some.

Life does take all day. There's not a spare minute in the day that is not consumed by the many tasks of survival. And tomorrow it starts all over again. It's little wonder that there seems to be a stuckness to life. We're not getting anywhere, 'cause we're barely keeping up. The whole village is in a perpetual state of hungry and tired. And the exhaustion is an open invitation to malaria.

It's also little wonder that invading armies find these villages easy victims. People struggle all day, so there's no fight left in them. One of the UN military observers in Kalemie remarked to me, "I don't think the war can restart; the people are exhausted." What the observer missed is that the people are always exhausted.

This may also explain why worship is so rich and deeply satisfying. Only in this kind of day-to-day struggle is the Sabbath so welcome, the joy so genuine, thanksgiving so heartfelt. They praise a God who is bigger than their village life.

Here's what I think: Africa Time is a cover for the awkwardness that exists when we Americans try to help Africans. It is an attempt to regain dignity lost, to reframe the embarrassment of need into a cultural explanation, to regain some sense of control.

When an American friend, trying to see a map of Africa in his mind, asked me how far the Congo was from South Africa, I responded, "About fifty years." He got it/didn't get it. When I told Ntambo this joke, he said, "Maybe a hundred years."

When he and I are talking peer to peer, Ntambo says simply that the Congo is fifty years behind in development, and he thinks in terms of fifty years as he institutes programs of change and development. He is starting universities with basic buildings, dreaming not of what they look like now, or even in his lifetime, but what they will be in fifty years, a hundred years.

There is some technological leapfrogging happening, what with cell phones in the jungle, but I think he has it about right. Furthermore, I think that this working assumption is much healthier than a cultural labeling that leaves Africans permanently in a primitive culture. Many social practices are not necessarily cultural, but rather temporal. When I visit an African village, I see my grandparents' farm life fifty years ago. The distance between them is as much in time as it is in geography. I remember the Saturdays when all my aunts and uncles showed up to work the harvest and we cousins played in the yard. There were chickens in that yard, chickens that were running around now but would soon be dinner. I remember my grandparents' outhouse, a two-holer. Now, whether global economic development is on the right track and whether more primitive cultures have much to teach us are two important, but different, questions.

Africa Time has a close corollary in Jesus Time. The Congolese people have fallen into the insanity of repeating the same action while expecting a different result. I contend that this practice is not cultural but rather historical and that it can be challenged and reversed. After the war, a wave of charity passed through the villages. UNICEF built schools and provided school supplies (even new classroom desks), and hope soared. UNICEF plastic school totes are everywhere. The new metal desks are found not only in classrooms but also now in homes. These are constant reminders to the community of the hope in which they live: the hope that another wave of charity is coming. When will it come? When Jesus comes. That's Jesus Time.

Jesus time is not a literal belief in Jesus's return, but a way of not thinking too much about the insanity of doing the same thing over and over again with the same result. It's always said with a laugh. The villagers of Mulongo remember when they had a United Methodist missionary. They want me to be their missionary. When will that happen? When Jesus comes.

Jesus Time.

Years ago, my Annapolis roommate, Don, introduced me to the cargo cults of Melanesia. In an article in the *Air Force Magazine* dated January 1991, C.V. Glines outlined the development of the cults, which can be traced to early sailing ships of Captain Cook. Accelerated by the air transport traffic of World War II, mixed with the evangelism of Christian missionaries laid upon traditional beliefs, confused by language misunderstandings and the isolation of the small islands, an apocalyptic religion grew, based on a belief that a deliverer was coming to bring the cargo that the community needed to bring it into a new prosperous age. One of the more curious discoveries was of an isolated community in the Solomons worshipping a photo of King George V as Ihova (God).

That's where the Congolese live. Even though they work very hard every day, their hope is vested in a future event where a Jesus-like coming brings the cargo they need. Missionaries and aid agencies reinforce this just often enough to keep the hope alive. This is why we at Friendly Planet Missiology are fundamentally opposed to packing our hand-me-downs in shipping containers and sending them to Africa. That's the perfect example of good people trying to help without an understanding of what that act is doing to a people theologically (and incidentally destroying the hitherto existing local clothing businesses). It's amazing how the church quits thinking theologically when it shifts into mission mode.

Jesus Time: A way to believe in a coming salvation while resigning yourself to the reality that it's never going to come, at least not to you and not in your lifetime. To have only one hope, and to cynically accept your hopelessness. Wow. Amen. And amen. Forever hopeless.

Sometimes I get a glimpse of this hopeful hopelessness on the bicycle. It's taking us all day to climb this mountain. I'm starting to think we'll get to Mwanza only in Jesus Time.

## Jesus Is the Answer?

*S*till climbing. Pushing the heavy bicycle up the mountain. Hot. Drenched in sweat. Fever. Other than that, feeling at one with the universe. May as well continue reflecting.

Speaking of Jesus, what does Jesus have to do with any of this? Actually, more than you think, but not at all what you think.

In the American frontier evangelism preached in Africa, I would say that Jesus is a fail. There is no more Christian a people than the Congolese. Every thought is phrased as a religious thought. Church is not only the center of community life, it is life itself. For every problem, Jesus is the answer.

But is Jesus the answer?

Bear with me. I'm looking at a world where Jesus is proclaimed as savior and people believe that Jesus is their savior, but something isn't right. It's not working.

There are at least two ways it's not working.

First, this is the rape capital of the world. And the corruption is everywhere. The lying and cheating and backstabbing. And all of this in the church itself.

Second, even for the faithful pure of heart, this isn't working. There's no good news. The Gospel is some kind of cruel joke.

I have to ask, does the Christian faith have a message that makes any sense here?

Set aside your passion for the Gospel for a moment and ask this probing question: Has Christianity helped or hurt, or has it simply given new names to old gods?

Is there a particular and peculiar message in the narrative of the life of Jesus that speaks to the struggles of these people?

I'm compelled to insist that in order to arrive at an answer that is helpful, we must first of all answer, "Maybe not."

Then sit with that possibility. For a long time. As long as it takes. And then some. Until it gets uncomfortable. Until it gets possible that we've all been wrong.

Personally, I've been sitting with this question since 1991, my first visit. At the time I thought that there could not be a more broken place. And yet I had never seen a more religious people. The knee-jerk daily devotional response would be to marvel at the faith in the midst of suffering. But that's not what I was seeing. There was some kind of disconnect—a disconnect I could not name.

Eventually, I came to see the disconnect in the patronage system in which people lived. Then I saw that same patronage system in historical Jesus studies from Albert Schweitzer to John Dominic Crossan. I had to sit in the middle of it to see it, but then I couldn't not see it.

## Question: Did Jesus address the issue of patronage in his time and place?

*A*nswer: Yes. He did. I would argue that it was not simply a side issue, but central to his message. When you sit inside a patronage system, all the kingdom of God sayings make sense.

So, then, Jesus is the answer, or rather, Jesus gave the answer. But you have to know the question.

In broad brushstrokes, here is the answer, or here are the answers:

1.   If you are going to have a patron, get a good patron, and God is the only good patron. This is what the *Our Father* (Matthew 6:9–13, Luke 11:2–4) is about. God is not our daddy, as in the male parent of a nuclear family. God is the patron. What convinced me of this is the way everybody who wants and needs something from me calls me "Father."

2.   You don't need a patron. "The kingdom of God is within you." (Luke 17:21) Walk away from the system. You don't need it. The first time I preached "Everything you need, God has already provided," I felt like a cold-hearted cad, saying such cruel things to people in the worst sort of poverty. The response was surprising. People heard this as good news. They came to me with all their best ideas and energy to get to work.

I'm fully aware that I'm proposing that we peel back the layers of tradition that created these texts, that this requires an imagining of Jesus speaking these teachings in a context that predates a later context of their writing. But sitting in these Congolese villages has given me a picture of a cultural setting where Jesus' original historic words make sense to the struggles that these people are facing in their daily lives.

Jesus is the answer. And Jesus Time is now.

# Mwanza

$A$s they tend to do in the eastern Congo, the mountain has become a plateau and the road has leveled, giving us a good 14 kilometers per hour, even though my legs feel like rubber. The push up the mountain was exhausting, and the sun is cooking us. We're just a few kilometers from Mwanza, and I'm tired, hot, and hungry. I'm ready to stop when we arrive at the town and its market, but no, we keep going. We stop at a United Methodist church on the far side of town and greet the pastor, but we're not done. The pastor joins us as we ride another couple of kilometers to the mission station and the district superintendent's house. The day's goalpost keeps moving.

The sun is scorching hot now, but we have to endure the welcoming ceremony. I'm standing, ready at any second to pass out, in front of the district superintendent's home, the old missionary house. I say that I am standing instead of saying we are standing. The rest of the team has moved over under the nearest tree for the shade while I'm left abandoned to this show of protocol, and the speeches are droning on. Everybody assumes I know what they are saying. I sort of do. I've heard this speech so many times. But it's hot! I've just climbed a mountain, put two gallons of sweat in my shirt, and left blood on the road. My legs are spent. My head is faint. I'm dying out here in the hot sun. Mad dogs and Englishmen.

When the speeches are over, we are welcomed into the house. The steps up to the house have been washed away in the seasons of rain, so it's a giant leap up to even get onto the concrete steps to the porch. Inside, the living room is furnished with bamboo chairs and chaise longues. This is a house straight out of a Joseph Conrad novel. We're invited to sit, and I do. Lunch will be served soon. Africa Time.

This house goes back several missionaries, and Delbert and Sandy Groves lived here. It's big. These old colonial houses look as if they have two stories, but it's just that the roofs are so high—for cooling, I guess. There's not much of a ceiling. Delbert had told me that there was no ceiling when he and Sandy arrived, and there's not much of a ceiling now, so whatever he had done didn't stick. The house looks more like a ruin than a house, but that's how Delbert described it the day they moved in. There's an old Land Rover sitting in the backyard, stripped during the war. I set up my bicycle against it and take a picture.

Mulongo is ambitious and wants to get to Kikondja, so we're not going to spend the night here. After the meal, though, we are taken on a tour of the mission station.

First we are shown the high school, an agricultural tech school. It looks to be in pretty good shape compared to most schools we've seen. Its solid construction has stood the test of time and seasons. The history I hear in the villages does not always match up with the history I've heard from missionaries. Our tour guide today says that the missionary Hammond had come here to build this school, which may well be the case. It could be wrong, though, and I may get letters from both missionaries and church leaders correcting me on this point. Delbert told me that Hammond had been in this village only one year, a year that Hammond said was the worst year of his life. I don't mean to tell tales out of school, just to point out that the worst year of a missionary's life might just go down as a lasting work in a community he or she served.

The heat from the sun feels as if it's directed straight at this village, making everything from rocks to scrub trees so inhospitable, but our walking tour continues. From the school, we climb along a wandering footpath to the clinic. I know from Delbert that there has been a clinic here for many years, but this is a new building, built by World Vision, which has a history of working closely with The United Methodist Church in this region. I'm told by missionaries that when World Vision first came to Zaire, it worked under the UMC until it could get its own NGO designation.

The problem with World Vision's new building for the United Methodist clinic in Mwanza is that this new clinic has no water, no electricity, no medicines. There are three nurses on staff, but no salaries. What a laboratory for missiology! Here stands an outpost clinic in a remote underserved region. Is this the ragged edge of the frontier of the mission of the church where the resources have run out, or is this a picture of the failure of our model?

First there's the issue of polity, or rather the polity perception gap, as I call it. The local community sees this clinic as a project of The United Methodist Church, so they wonder why The United Methodist Church is not providing any funding. Unfortunately, no one in America has thought of this mission station in years, and this lonely clinic isn't even on the radar of The United Methodist Church, which has a new, and huge, initiative to wipe out diseases of poverty, including malaria and HIV/AIDS. This clinic is not a part of the big new plan.

Then there's the issue of self-sufficiency. Perhaps it is reasonable to expect the local community to pony up for the water, electricity, medicines, and salaries, having been given the building. From the donor side, that might make sense. Standing here, it looks like a cruel joke. If that were the plan, someone should have informed the community. I have a lot more to learn before I can know how much of the burden of the delivery of health care can be carried by this poor village.

We're standing just outside the front door of the clinic, high on the mountain. While I've been thinking these thoughts about the perception of responsibility, Mulongo has been trying to get a signal for his cell phone. If there is a signal, this is the place to stand. His call reaches Bishop Ntambo, who has been tracking us and wants to know how I am doing. It dawns on me that the bishop is still anxious for my well-being. If something happens to me, he loses face, and maybe worse. No matter how many times I tell him that he is not responsible for my safety, in his mind, he is. I also realize that the bishop wants me to visit projects like the clinic at Mwanza, which is his project, unfunded and forgotten though it may be. He is having his own tug-of-war with the general church agencies concerning how best to serve North Katanga, and he wants me to be his witness. Bishop Ntambo is transforming from a beggar under the table of The United Methodist Church to a force to be reckoned with.

We don't spend any more time in Mwanza because Mulongo has plans to get beyond Kikondja to Kabenga before nightfall, where the district superintendent of the Kabenga District is waiting to host us. We're having some trouble keeping up with the itinerary that Mulongo has set for us. The villagers' goodwilled hospitality and their need to grab a patron for their projects causes each stop to be longer than planned. In an honor/shame motivated culture, one is constantly weighing the need to stay in the present village and respect the hospitality over and against the need to get to the next appointment on time so as to not shame the waiting responsible host. It doesn't matter much to me—as I said, as long as I get on that plane for spring break, I don't care how long we tarry in a given village—but it matters to Mulongo. This is the biggest expedition of his life, and he is responsible. He will go on to do much bigger and more important things, but this expedition will make his career.

# Mwanza to Kikondja

*S*habana and Éléphant came up the road from Malemba to catch up with us in Mwanza, but we still haven't heard from Prospère. We pick up another pastor as a guide.

The Michelin map—not the map I got from the Institut Geographique, but the color-coded road map of southern Africa I used before I found the Institut map—marks the road from Mwanza to Kikondja as "preferred bypass." Preferred to what? Bypass to what? It's clear no one from Michelin has made a site visit here in fifty years. The riding itself is not bad, but there's not a bridge on this road that hasn't been washed out, and it's slow going. We're along a ridgeline still, running roughly parallel with the Congo River but high enough above it and far enough from it that we can't see the river itself. To the south, toward the river, the landscape falls off and we can see for miles. Turning and looking north, we can only see the hillside.

The road is fairly flat, but the rivers are swollen and difficult to cross. The bridges we do see are surrounded by the water of the swollen rivers. We get plenty of local help in fording these rivers. Some strong young man lifts my bike over his head and carries it across rushing waters up to his armpits. He insists on carrying me. I insist on wading myself. I may not be able to lift my bicycle above my head and cross this river, but I want to maintain some dignity. There's that shame thing again. Besides that, the water is cool and cooling to the fever. When we get to the other side, the gathered crowd cheers and waves us a supportive "*Twenda muzuri!*" (Travel well!) "*Bakia muzuri,*" we wave back. (Stay well.) This drama recurs every 5 or 10 kilometers. It's clear that no truck is going to make it down this road until dry season.

A delight of the day: We do cross a river fork, where two streams meet. Three young boys are in the water, sitting in the spot where the two streams come together. Éléphant points out that one stream is cold water while the other flows from a hot spring. I wish we had time to stop for some hot tub time.

## Cargo Cults and Plebe Year

*I* want to talk more about the patronage system. It is key to understanding what is happening here. However, I want now to go back to my own pre-patronage understanding, before I had a word for it. Let me go back to those cargo cults I mentioned when talking about Africa Time. The article my Annapolis roommate, Don, sent me, written for those interested in military history, was my first introduction to this strange religious phenomena in the islands of the South Pacific, but it moved me to deeper theological scholarship, especially the work of British anthropologist Peter Worsley.

When I first arrived in the DR Congo (then called Zaire), back in the early 1990s, my mind was filled with thoughts of the cargo cults, and I saw them everywhere. It was clear to me at the time that I was looking at one giant cargo cult. Two problems jumped right out at me.

First, despite the missionaries' own understanding of what they were preaching, there was a not so subliminal message in their evangelism. Salvation comes from outside the community, and it comes in a white face. Regardless of their words, the visual message was way too strong to overcome. I would argue that this is even more the case when the evangelism requires a total conversion away from all things traditional. The message then becomes, "Nothing here is good; all good things come from outside. Old is bad, new is good, and the giver of this new and good is a white outsider."

Second, the missionary feeds the belief that the salvation from poverty comes from outside. Missionaries bring their households and all ministry supplies in shipping containers. They are themselves the ultimate cargo cult. What locals see is that the solution arrives in a container. The almost hilarious outcome is that the goal of all missionary projects then becomes movement toward self-sufficiency. We seem so surprised that the community falls into dependency, and we blame the people for their dependent nature, finding a cultural character flaw that must be converted. All along, the mission model delivers exactly what it logically must—a cargo cult.

When I was in my plebe year at the U.S. Naval Academy with Don, our interactions with upperclassmen and officers was constrained by tradition. A plebe is allowed to give one of only five answers. It could be a sermon: "Everything I Know about Leadership, I Learned Plebe Year." I could link it to Jesus' "Let your yes be yes, and your no be no." (Matthew 5:37) Yes, seminarians, I'm fully aware that this is blatant eisegesis, but there you go.

The first two answers are straightforward:

Answer #1: "Yes, sir." This is the positive response to a yes or no question. Straight yes or no, no waffle language, no rambling, no additional words required. Anything beyond yes begins to build a lie.

Answer #2: "No, sir." This is the negative response to a yes or no question. See #1.

Answer #3: "Aye, aye, sir." This is the answer to a direct order. It means, "I understand your command, and I will comply. I will do it." Again, there is no waffle language. Note that for the plebe, there is no negative equivalent. However, in the course of four years at the U.S. Naval Academy, midshipmen will encounter countless case studies of how a subordinate responds to an unlawful order and the subject will be fully debated. I would argue that it is the stewardship of this built-in conflict in the code of conduct that defines one truly as a commissioned officer, or in the church, an ordained clergyperson.

This conflict is reflected in a ritual exchange: When plebes are asked the question "What's up?" the required answer is, "Sir, Fidelity is up and Obedience is down." Those who live in Bancroft Hall know that this answer is in reference to the parade belt buckle. The words *Fidelity* and *Obedience* are stamped on the belt buckle. To get it right side up, ensure that the word *Fidelity* is on top and *Obedience* is on the bottom. Beyond getting your belt on correctly, the true leader is the one who holds in trust the relationship between fidelity to the greater good and obedience to the rules of the community. In the long run, fidelity trumps obedience.

Answer #4: "No excuse, sir." This is the heart of plebe training. It is the hardest lesson to learn, and it is the taproot of all codes of life for the naval officer. "No excuse" is the taking on of the consequences of your actions, the actions of those under your command, and even the actions of classmates and shipmates. It includes even acts of God, storms of nature, and accidents you had absolutely no control over. It is so far beyond taking responsibility for your own actions that you are silently absorbing the failures of all around you. If one were a Christian, one might begin to get an inkling of an idea of the meaning of atonement. The good news is that on the other side of this discipline comes a freedom unknown to those who go through life trying to explain themselves and their every action. The other great discovery is that those above you on the chain of command know exactly what you are saying, or what you are not saying when you are silent. The perceived (from the outside) downside to this discipline is what folks might call "falling on your sword." It is why the captain of a ship is relieved of command, or worse, even when it is clear to all that a subordinate was at fault. My wife has never made peace with this code.

Back when we were second class midshipmen (sophomores) at the U.S. Naval Academy, Don and I were qualifying for command of the famous YPs, the yard patrol craft that operated on the Severn River and into the Chesapeake Bay. Weighing in at 80 tons on 80 feet of waterline, these miniature destroyers are not so small. I had spent my high school summers in Indiana driving a John Deere 4020, and I love the smell of diesel in the morning! The twin screw, the twin rudder, and four Detroit Diesels in the engine room (five counting the generator) put power at your control. Well, almost at your control. The conning officer in training on the open bridge of a YP does not have direct control of the ship. All control is by voice command through old-fashioned voice tubes. This is old-school boat driving.

We had been out in the bay running imaginary (and unauthorized) torpedo runs at the supertankers, who were totally unaware of the threat we were presenting them. The weather was classic Chesapeake Bay winter: cold, wet, and windy. The seas were choppy to rough. It was a great day to be at sea! We were filled with the testosterone of junior naval officers joyriding without concern for the responsibility of command.

When we returned to the naval station dock, there were the obligatory "bumper drills." Like learning to land an airplane, docking a boat is a skill that is never fully mastered, and is forever practiced. It takes a day to learn how to fly. It takes a lifetime to learn how to land. Same for boats.

Don went first. His landing was ugly, hampered by uncooperative wind and current, but it was, in truth, a textbook landing. It just looked ugly. Aesthetics are important, especially when two friends are competing for best boat handler. I determined to learn from his ugly landing and make mine art. The key would be to hold more speed into the wind and make the 80 tons slide into the dock in one beautiful maneuver. Timing the reversal of the engines would be the key.

With the swagger of Lt. Kennedy at the con of PT-109, I brought the YP smartly around and lined it up perfectly for the landing. (As John Paul Jones said, "Give me a fast ship for I intend to go in harm's way.")

From Don's attempt, I knew the angle of attack I needed into this wind. When everything was lined up and the speed was strong enough to beat the wind and current, slicing through the angry waves, I called out orders down to the wheelhouse: "Rudder amidships, all engines stop." I was going to coast the perfect landing right up to the dock and kiss it sweetly.

But something went wrong, terribly wrong. We weren't slowing. The engines were still engaged. I could feel it in my feet on the steel deck. No panic, though. There was still time to correct. "All engines back one-third."

That's when the bells in the engine room went off, the bells that alert everyone on board that the engine controls in the engine room are in the opposite direction of the engine order telegraph (yeah, we were still using that ancient nautical device) in the wheelhouse.

My next command was the highlight of my naval career. "Hard left rudder, all engines back full," and then I said them, those famous words, those once in a life-time (if ever) words, those words only a rare few captains get to say for real in a career: "Standby to ram!"

And ram we did. We broke through every 16-by-16 piece of timber on that dock. Waterlines and electrical conduit were sliced, creating water fountains and fire-works. Sailors ran for cover. Oh, you should have been there. What a show!

Teri makes certain that when I tell this story, I tell people about the plebe in the engine room asleep at the throttle, but that's not the point. No excuse. I could blame it on the plebe in the engine room, but that was something I would have to take up with him in private. In public, this was my shipwreck.

As a side note, fortunately for me, but unfortunately for him, a lieutenant com-mander was on board as a safety officer. We midshipmen had to get a commis-sioned officer to sign for the YP before taking it out. I hope it didn't harm his career. I suspect it was written off as normal training damage, expected of a couple of twenty year olds. The YP itself was barely scratched, which leads me to believe that they were built with this probability in the specs.

Don uses this story as cachet in the swapping of war stories at Lockheed Martin. I use it as an introduction in the first sermon I preach at a new appointment. It gives the folks a chance to laugh at me, and down the road, when I want to preach on peace building, the veterans give me a listen.

What does this have to do with pastors in the Congo? Everything, I contend. At least two things, anyway. OK, one thing.

Every plan for development—even systems thinking, of which I am a big fan—begins with determining the cause of the problem and fixing the problem at the cause. That makes sense, so far. However, this leads to the blame game. In the Congo, it takes only a few steps to get to colonial oppression, or government cor-ruption, or multinational corporations' rape of the minerals, or Rwanda's invasion. All of these are spot on, but not necessarily helpful to the local village leader. The cause of my shipwreck was someone else's mistake in a different part of the ship; nonetheless, the responsibility was mine on the bridge.

Let's consider for a moment the possibility that a solution to a problem doesn't have to be related to the cause. Theologically, this may be the practical application of forgiveness. What if we stopped looking at the cause and started looking only for a workable solution, recognizing that the solution we are looking for may not be even remotely related to the cause? Throw out cause and effect for a moment to open up a whole new box of possibilities.

First, we would let go of the emotional energy directed at those who have caused us this pain. I'm not forgetting justice, but I'm going to have to let someone else take care of the bad guys. Maybe the World Court, maybe SEAL Team Six, maybe God. I'll probably never come to a peace with my rage against all the crooked, greedy cheats of the world, from corrupt despots to my own colleagues who are systematically destroying institutions that I cherish, and getting paid handsomely to do it. I have to set aside my jealousies and frustrations with denominational leaders, just as the Congolese local leaders have to set aside their justified anger with corrupt politicians and greedy multinational corporations. I'm probably more upset with do-gooders who are prospering while the poor suffer even more, and who get honored on the news for their philanthropy, than I am with obvious evil people. The obvious evil people present no disguise.

Second, we would be able to see the possibilities in front of us. During one visit to Kamina, Bishop Ntambo took me out to meet a local farmer. After her Belgian husband had died, this Congolese woman continued to live on the farm and run it. And run it she did. In addition to growing staples like cassava and maize, she experimented with all kinds of crops, including coffee. We enjoyed breakfast in her garden, the finest coffee and fruit trays. She did not have a tractor but a team of cows for plowing the fields, and she employed several dozen farm laborers. Madame Rachel was one classy lady, a smart businesswoman, and a hard worker.

As we were looking over a newly plowed field, Bishop Ntambo kicked a dirt clod and said, "Let them have the gold. We have this." He was making a simple point: While the whole world is killing for the minerals in the ground, we're overlooking the earth itself. We have arable land, and lots of it—no need for commercial fertilizer even. We have sunshine and rain, both in abundance. We can do two maize crops a year, and three peanut crops a year.

Many village markets are stocked with rice from Vietnam. What's that about? This place should be not only feeding all of its people, but it should also be exporting food, not importing it. This should be a breadbasket for Africa, if not for the world.

Being focused on the war for minerals is causing us to miss the other resources—not only agriculture, but so many other resources. The Congo River drops a mile on its way from the Zambian border to the Atlantic. Along the way, in hundreds of tributaries, are powerful waterfalls, enough so that every house in the Congo should have free electricity generated by these falls. It is a gift of God. Also, the mountains are so full of limestone and gypsum that cement should be a leading export, but we are importing cement from Zambia and Tanzania. The textile industry of the Congo was once famous. Before the standard was Egyptian cotton, it was Congolese cotton.

The list goes on and on. From beer to tourism, so many Congolese assets are left underdeveloped. This is indeed the richest country in the world with the world's poorest people, even without the gold, coltan, uranium, tin, copper, cobalt, and diamonds. The obvious cause of all this poverty is the mismanagement of what is a potential of a trillion dollars a year, but if those at the big boys' table won't get their acts together to lead the nation toward both peace and prosperity, what's the local leader supposed to be doing?

In speaking with local community leaders, I often open with saying to them, "I know that this is not your fault. You didn't cause it, but you're the one who is going to have to fix it." If we wait until we can get the bad guys to confess and change their ways, it's not going to happen, and because the bad guys include the courts, the businesspeople, and the international community, there's nowhere to take our complaint. Even those who are trying to help out with their charity are making things worse. So it falls to us. It falls to local leaders who have no money, who have no support, and who will get no recognition, because we are working against the model.

It's just us, because as Travis said to Crockett at the Alamo, "Sam Houston's not coming." (Do I have to footnote this? Because I have no idea if this is true. It just sounds true.)

So we begin. We can start by taking advantage of the resources that the big boys are ignoring while they fight over the mines. We can find ways to leverage these lesser resources—resources that would be considered major resources in any other country—into a working economy, an economy that is working well at the village level.

That was a lengthy reflection on "No excuse, sir," Plebe Answer #4. Let's move on to that last answer.

Answer #5: "I'll find out, sir." This is the answer to any question of content learning. "What's the name of the navy's F4 fighter?" "What's for lunch?" The answer is never "I don't know." If you don't know, find out. And the next time you're asked, you'll know. This is not as deep a leadership discipline as Answer #4, but it is an excellent work habit to develop. In a counterintuitive way, it builds self-confidence and self-esteem. It also fits well into FPM's missiological process. We don't teach content. We provoke leaders to research answers.

I can't fix Africa. I have neither the resources nor the authority to command all the players. Lacking resources and political power, I am forced to find a better plan and a better way to live.

# Kikondja to Kabenga

*W*hen we get to Kikondja, we pick up another rider. I think he's a pastor. He has trouble keeping up, so I don't get to know him. His bicycle keeps losing its chain. He stops and puts it back on, then rides like the devil to catch up.

The road moves into a forest. We're under the canopy, and the air is almost pleasant, a bit moist. Our guide from behind, on the broken bicycle, keeps telling us that it's only 10 kilometers or so to go. Ten kilometers doesn't seem like much, but the pace has slowed in the forest because the road wide enough to be used by trucks consists of water holes and mounds of mud. We climb above the road to follow a trail through the bush, but the rideable path is essentially a single track. There are roots, mud, and the stubs of small broken trees. Occasionally, the panniers get snagged.

My colleagues are keeping pace on this upper track, but I'm finding it too technical and too difficult. Thank God for the new guy on the bad bike who keeps me from being the one slowing down the group.

It's a lot more than 10 kilometers from Kikondja to Kabenga, where we are scheduled to stop tonight. I'd like to romanticize this ride and call it my dark night of the soul, but there is no spiritual reflecting going on. This is my night from hell.

It starts to rain. First, it's gentle and refreshing. Then it turns hard and annoying. Big drops are collecting on my glasses, blurring my vision. I try to wipe my glasses, but that doesn't work. And looking down with the bifocals just makes the blurring worse. Eventually, I just take off the glasses and put them in my shirt pocket. I can't see well without them, but I wasn't seeing anyway. I pull my Red Sox cap down tight, and the bill protects the top of my face. I put on my rain jacket. It's worthless. Better to be soaked. The team is still moving at pace. I'm cursing every root that jumps off the trail to grab my tire. I'm doing my best to keep up, in the rain, on the single track full of roots and ruts that I can't see. And the team keeps moving at pace.

The sun goes down. Darkness sneaks up on me under the canopy. At least the darkness fixes my eyesight. Now I really can't see. I have a headlight. I turn it on.

According to the instructions, I should get one hour of service on high, but ten hours on low. Of course, I chose low. I have a charger for this light, but it's 110 volts. Nowhere for the rest of the trip will I be able to recharge this headlight. This is going to be a use once and done. This is the night to use it.

Mulongo made a commitment not to ride at night, and so far, we haven't, much. A little getting in at dusk, but so far, no night riding. We have no choice; we're night riding tonight.

Always, it's just ten kilometers more. Hours later, ten to go. I finally give in to the unavoidable truth: This is my eternity. I make peace with the rain. I make peace with the dark. I make peace with the road. I find a pace that I can ride forever, because this is forever. Maybe this is the dark night of my soul. I had arrived at such a level of peace that when word is passed back that we are approaching the village, I'm not ready to stop riding. I no longer want to stop.

It is midnight when we arrive in the village of Kabenga, a full six hours after we had been expected. The welcoming party had long ago gone to bed. It is pouring rain and not a fit night out for anyone. All of the villagers are hunkered down in the driest places they can find because the rain is pouring even inside their huts.

The pastor and his wife are there to greet us. In the dark, they escort us into a small house, into a small room with a candle and a table. It is actually a little chilly, and we could have used a fire to dry by, but there is no way to dry. Hot water is brought for tea or coffee. I now know what an incredible act of hospitality that had to be to heat the water in that downpour.

After the coffee and tea, we are led to the church. It is astonishing! The church is huge! Even in the dark I can tell that this is a big church. I am later told that Bishop wa Kadilo built this church back in the 1980s. Although Bishop wa Kadilo had built the exterior of this church in the 1980s, the interior still is unfinished. When I had met the pastor and his wife at the annual conference in Kamina the year before, they complained to me that they were being sent to this village as punishment, and they couldn't understand how the bishop could hate them so. Over warm drinks in the rain on this night, they thank me for the farming tools we had provided at the conference, saying, "You saved our lives." They are dying there. They don't deserve this.

We pitch our tents on the dirt floor under the dry of the church's tin roof to go to sleep. I marvel at the size of this church in a poor village where the pastor and his wife are dying from lack of income and food, from exhaustion and disease, and mostly from isolation. There are pastors who are builders. This pastor is not one. He's not going to survive out here.

# *Kabenga to Nyembo*

The rains in Kabenga stop by morning, and we are on the road again. Destination: Nyembo Mpungu. Nyembo was the site of the 1995 North Katanga Annual Conference, my first gig as a keynote preacher. There, I unveiled the first drafts of "Preaching Revelation in Africa," which was my first attempt to use Scripture as a code to reflect back to the community its generative themes. The images of horror and terror in Revelation matched the horror and terror in the cities and villages of the Congo. I did not have to say, "This is what this text means." They knew exactly what the text meant. They were living it. I wasn't preaching some prediction of God-initiated future events. I was telling them about their present, using the biblical texts, not literal but real.

The annual conference in Nyembo in 1995 was also where we unveiled the bicycle project. Ntambo had said to me, "When you come, bring 200 bicycles." This was the beginning of a beautiful working relationship. I raised the $25,000 in Indiana, the first $5,000 from the church I was pastoring, then the rest just rolled in effortlessly from around the state. We asked for $125 for a bicycle, bite-size for a family or a Sunday school class. Easiest money I ever raised.

The decisions around the bicycle project set our missiology for all projects to come. We said "no thanks" to those who wanted to clean out their garages and give us old bicycles to be shipped to Zaire. We decided that we would not go into the container business. Instead, we would buy the bicycles locally, in Lubumbashi, from local businesses. The logic was that in doing so, we would stimulate the local economy. Also, repair parts for locally sourced bicycles would be available in secondary markets.

So, Ntambo and I went from store to store in Lubumbashi buying bicycles, four here, eight there, until we had 200. This did, indeed, stimulate the local economy. The next year, when we went shopping for bicycles, every store had loads of them. In one year, the new bicycle availability went from scarce to plentiful.

The bicycles were made in India, labeled *Kinga,* a multilingual pun using the Swahili word for *bicycle* and a crown logo playing off the English word *king.* And each one came with a tool kit, a light, and a rear rack. Most of the accessories failed early, but the frames were strong and had a half-life of about ten years. They were good, solid, standard, single-speed world bicycles. Perfect.

Still in pieces in their boxes, the bicycles had to be trucked up to the annual conference sites, 150 to Nyembo and 50 to Manono for the Tanganyika-Tanzania Annual Conference. We paid mechanics $3 a bike for assembly, and the sight of 150 bicycles being built at the annual conference was inspiring. The bicycle distribution ceremony drew a crowd from all over. The bishop's cabinet had met to determine which appointments required bicycles, and congregations came to watch their pastors receive them. Pastors' spouses sang and danced for joy with each gift.

As the conference came to a close, and the pastors scattered to their appointments, there were parades of United Methodist pastors on bicycle on the roads through the villages. The next year, it was reported that 95 babies were delivered by these bicycles. (That's an awkward statement, but you know what I mean.) On speaking tours in America, Ntambo likened the gift of a bicycle to the gift of a Boeing 747.

This distribution of bicycles was repeated the next year, but 1995 is remembered as the year everything changed. Old pastors tell me that they were there for the big bicycle distribution and that that's where they received their first bicycles. The conferences became truly itinerant that year. Pastors now had transportation, and I believe that this was the first time something this big had been done specifically for the equipping of pastors for their work.

Many years later, a pastor by the name of Gertrude was selected to spend a semester at Wesley Theological Seminary in Washington, DC, as part of an Africa University study abroad program. She became friends with my daughter Taylor, who was also studying at Wesley. Taylor put her on a bus to Indiana to spend a weekend at our house. Gertrude sat down with Teri and told her this story:

"When I was a new pastor, I received one of those bicycles. I was shy at the time and couldn't speak English, so I couldn't thank Baba Bob for the bicycle, but it made my ministry possible. Before, I had nothing. The bicycle was the beginning of my work. When Taylor came to Kamina, years later, I was living in Kamina, but I still did not have the courage to approach her to thank her. Now I am in your home. God has brought me all the way here just to thank you, Mama Teri. God has brought me a long way, and it began with that bicycle."

Gertrude is now a lecturer at Africa University in Zimbabwe.

When we got to Manono to repeat the distribution, a missionary friend, a good guy, said to me, "This is a nice thing you have done for them." Ntambo, on the same day, said to me, "This is the most important thing we have done in thirty years." Hear the difference? Both were true and positive statements about the project. One gave me credit for a nice thing. In the other statement, Ntambo took credit for delivering an essential tool that was going to transform the pastors' work. He deserved all the credit. He had the vision. He did the work. He delivered the goods. All I did was raise the $25,000, the easy part, and show up for the party. This set the mold for our work together. We've pulled off a lot of good projects since, and they've all had this same formula.

It was here to Nyembo that I brought Taylor and two teenage brothers in 1995. Maybe, more accurately, they tagged along as I was brought to Nyembo. I certainly didn't know where we were going. There I was in Nyembo, still technically a war zone, with three teenagers, and I hadn't a clue as to what I was doing. We were totally dependent upon our Congolese hosts. Here is where I abandoned my daughter and her companions to return home on their own while I stayed to continue on to Manono.

When the three teenagers got back to their classes at Lawrence Central High School, they were required to write those essays, "What I Did on Summer Vacation and How It Changed My Life." The two boys wrote perfectly fine essays. Mostly, the essays were about how, now that they had seen how the rest of the world lives, they are thankful for the privileges and opportunities they enjoy as Americans. Perfectly fine. And the two boys ended up doing good stuff in life. One earned a PhD in political science and teaches in Hong Kong. The other works for the Salvation Army. Good boys. Glad I took them. I think they were changed.

Taylor, on the other hand, wrote a completely different essay: "Wow, what beautiful people and what a wonderful place. I'm going to live there one day." And so she set out to do just that, earning a master's degree in international development at American University in Washington, DC, and moving to Kamina to work for Bishop Ntambo, where he appointed her head of the department of community development for the North Katanga Conference. I took her to the Congo in 2005 and left her there, the second time as a father I took my daughter into a war zone and abandoned her there. Bad father. That being said, had Taylor not had the passion to return to the Congo to live and work there, I would have never returned myself. It was Taylor who brought me back here.

When we arrive in Nyembo on our bicycles in 2010, we don't get much of a reception. There's no welcome parade and no worship and no dog and pony show. It's a place to stop that has *mzungu*-style accommodations. Mulongo and I are put up in the old house of the missionaries John and Kendra Enright, who left in the evacuation of 1998. Although the house legally belongs to the conference, it is still furnished with the Enrights' furniture with family photos still hanging on the walls. They are now living in Ndola, Zambia, and I don't know if they intend to return. It's a long story and not mine to tell. The house has been closed up since they left, and it's opened only for the rare occasion of someone like me showing up. It's maintained move-in ready, still waiting for the return of the missionaries, whether they are the Enrights or someone else. The master bedroom is padlocked, and we stay in one of the boys' bedrooms.

After we settle in, there is a short tour. We ride over to the church side of the mission. By church side, I mean that there is a clear "other side of the tracks" layout of the campus. There's no track, but there is a missionary side and a church side. There are two worlds: the world of the missionaries and the world of the Congolese church leaders. It's modeled (unconsciously?) after the model for all Congolese towns, a side for the Africans (where the town name ends in *–cité*) and a side for the Europeans (where the town name ends in *–ville*).

John Enright had built a first class conference center here, complete with a super-sized assembly hall, housing for visitors, and a lumber business to fund it. Electricity was generated by a turbine embedded in the waterfall. We don't go see any of that.

I'm curious about the house where we stayed in 1995, which belonged to the Crows, missionaries from Ohio. We don't go see that, either.

# Don't Ask, Don't Tell

*T*his is where the discipline of deep listening gets hard. I'm aware that my curiosity is piqued, but I know that it is piqued about *mzungu* stuff. Just because I'm curious doesn't mean that I should ask the question. I need to sit on my questions and listen. Listen for what the community wants me to know. I'm calling it my own "don't ask, don't tell" policy. I don't ask questions. I don't tell people answers.

There are two good reasons not to ask questions. The first is that as soon as I ask a question, I own the problem. The community is quick to turn its problems over to the outsider who shows an interest. The second is that when I ask questions, I get the answers that people expect me to want to hear, or the answer that the last missionary or aid worker who came through town was pushing. Sometimes, a lot of times, I'll get the answer that I just gave in a sermon last Sunday.

One week in Kalemie I happened to be worshiping with the same congregation on back-to-back Sundays. The sermon I preached the first Sunday was the choir anthem the second Sunday. First of all, that is so cool! Secondly, that ups the ante on sermons. Better than a podcast, the sermon takes on a life of its own and becomes a part of the community's story lore.

It's not that I don't have something good to teach, but the discipline in deep listening is to go deeper than my present understanding. If I want to know what the community is thinking, I cannot ask questions merely out of curiosity. While my wisdom can make a contribution, it is nothing compared to the power of the community's wisdom, once awakened. I am listening for the community's wisdom. Thus, I am learning to check my curiosity. This sounds so counterlogical, but when a question pops up in my brain, I check to see if it is simply my curiosity. Surprisingly, it almost always is. So I sit on that question. The drill is to kill all my questions in order to hear the community's deepest questions.

Curiosity isn't the only kind of question I try to avoid. There's also that question that isn't a question but a means of showing off knowledge, usually coming from our need to make sure that others see us as worthy to be in the conversation. In the classroom, we called the students who asked these questions "spring butts." (Maybe here we could call them "springboks.") I catch myself, every once in a while, chiming into a conversation just to let the others know that I understand what is being talked about in French or Swahili. Shame on me. I usually embarrass myself by revealing my ignorance and breaking the momentum of the discussion. It's better to keep my mouth shut. Listen.

There is something in my personality that lends itself to listening rather than talking. I was always the quiet child. My first structured experience with the discipline of silence was in Webelos, that transition from Cub Scouts to Boy Scouts. They took us out into the woods where we each spent the night by ourselves. We were probably spaced out along the ridge in shouting distance from one another, but it sure felt alone in the woods in the dark. I'm pretty sure that that was a snake that crawled up under my sleeping bag to sleep in my body heat. After the night alone, we spent a day without talking. It seemed that all the other boys were frustrated by this exercise and couldn't wait until the day was done. I was energized by it and wanted more.

Then there was Plebe Year at the U.S. Naval Academy. Except in our own dorm room, in the classroom, or on the athletic field, we did not talk, and had only those five answers for any questions asked us. Remember the five answers? Spend a year like that and you become aware of and annoyed by all the worthless chatter in the world. That was the point. Jesus said, "Let your yes be yes, and your no be no. All else is evil," or something like that.

## Nyembo to Kabondo Dianda

*I*t's only 30 kilometers from Nyembo Umpungu to Kabondo Dianda, and the road is fast. I've made this ride before. Back in 1995 when we delivered all those bicycles at Nyembo, I was invited to take a ride to Kabondo Dianda to visit the church there. We pulled half a dozen newly built bikes from the stable, and a group of pastors, including me, took off on a quick 30 kilometer bike ride with a 30 kilometer return. I made two big mistakes. One, I didn't get the saddle height adjusted right for me and assumed that on such a short ride it wouldn't be a big deal. It was a big deal. Even though I was in good riding shape, the poor fit punished my knees. Two, I wore blue jeans to ride in. The seams on the seat of my jeans wore huge sores on my bum. With aching knees and a sore bum, I had trouble walking for the next several days. My pride made me hide the pain, but I was hurting. On a perfectly tuned and fitted bicycle and with a well-conditioned bum on a perfect leather saddle, the ride to Kabondo Dianda now is a piece of cake. We get there in time for the full meal that had been prepared for us.

Coming into to town, though, is not so easy. We are held up by a big parade with bands and flags and lots of women marching.

"What's this?"

"It's International Women's Day."

Ever since, I've been aware when International Women's Day rolls around on the calendar. There aren't any parades on International Women's Day in the United States, but around the world it is a big deal. In Kabondo Dianda it's a big deal.

So I'm sitting on the front porch of the district parsonage in Kabondo Dianda watching the world in front of me. Beyond is the church. It's old, missionary era. Here's a new problem. While there is a great need for building new churches in this rapidly growing conference, the old churches are showing their age. This one has major structural cracks.

There's a tractor under the shade of a tree. All parts are in place, but I can't tell if it is in working condition. I'm watching a boy standing on the tractor seat, picking leaves from the tree, when I recognize it as the moringa tree that is trending right now in all the mission magazines. This miracle tree is touted to be the hope for all that ails Africa. Every part of this tree seems to be a cure for something. Cooking classes are taught on how to integrate the moringa leaves, roots, and bark into the family diet.

I'm impressed that the district superintendent has such a tree and is up on the latest development innovation. I say to him, "I see you have a moringa tree!" I'm all proud of my spotting the tree. "Oh, we've always had them" was his response.

Here's a lesson. I thought that the moringa tree was a new introduction. The way the magazines talked about it, I thought it had been brought from India or China as a new idea. It's been a part of folk medicine here forever. It is the West that has just now discovered it. So we have a bit of folk knowledge that has been suppressed by the push to introduce modern medicine. Now we want to reverse that push to go back to more natural medicines.

This sets me to thinking about the history created by the teaming of evangelism and medicine in the missionary era.

# *Witchcraft*

Nyembo is home to the tomb of Bishop Ngoy wa Kadilo, who died in 1995, between the time he had invited me to come speak at the annual conference and the time of the annual conference. When I heard that he had died, I said to myself, "There goes my invitation," but the invitation stuck and I went to Nyembo. It was a troubled time for the conference leadership. Half of the leadership, those of Bishop wa Kadilo's family, were convinced that the other half had poisoned him. On one hand, I doubt it, but on the other hand, it happens often enough for that to be possible. Bishop Ntambo, to this day, will not drink any drink not opened in his sight, or eat food that is not prepared by his own cook.

There's a whole underworld of intrigue and witchcraft[3] here, overlaid with a veneer of Christianity. I am so thankful that Marti Steussy, my Old Testament prof, made us get deep under the layers of our Western Christian assumptions to discover a whole prebiblical world, rich with spiritual energy and conflict. Every once in a while, when worship breaks away from its Western church constraints, I can see into that world.

I see two kinds of Congolese preachers here. The first is the kind that proclaims Christianity as a total break with the past. Conversion is complete. For many missionaries and their converts, Christianity is a war on witchcraft, and this war extends beyond the church. Traditional medicine = witchcraft; Western medicine = Christianity. The problem is that there is not enough Western medicine to go around, and the little that is available destroys self-sufficiency. An unsustainable model is destroying ancient knowledge.

On more than one occasion, though, I've been asked, "Why do we have to get rid of our pre-Christian tradition while you get to keep yours?" The Congolese pastors are more than aware of this and are rapidly adopting our Christmas trees, knowing more about their pagan origins than we do.

---

[3] I use the word *witchcraft,* even though I'm certain there is a more culturally correct word, because witchcraft carries the meaning that both Congolese and Americans understand in common.

The other kind of preacher I find is one who is more relaxed about traditional beliefs and sees them as old customs to be outgrown rather than fought against. They see their Christian faith in a spiritual stream that began with traditional beliefs and practices. There is a continuity and not a complete break. They speak of the ancient beliefs with respect even as they critique them. They respect the local traditional healer, the witch doctor, even as they present an alternative faith story. There is loving respect for the old ways, maybe because there is loving respect for the ancient ones in the village, and maybe because part of the longing is a return to the almost forgotten days before the world was so messed up by colonization.

Lest I defend witchcraft, let me acknowledge that a ton of harm is done to people through bad medical practices and a ton more of social power abuses, like rape and the general devaluation of women, who are kept in place through a system empowered by witchcraft. Local warlords use witchcraft to energize an insane level of violence.

Bishop Ntambo seems to me to represent the latter group. He values his traditional tribal roots and sees his Christian faith as complementary to his traditions. That's not to say he wants to continue in the old practices, but he does not speak disrespectfully of them. He loves to tell the story of his grandfather witch doctor and his grandfather's cannibalism. Even today, witchcraft is an active issue in the church. In Kalemie last year, Bishop Ntambo had to sit down with the leadership of a local congregation and rule on a case of the charge of witchcraft in the church.

Even those who oppose witchcraft believe in its power. My gut tells me, however, that missionaries and preachers who are pushing the war with witchcraft are having a tougher sell than those who are gently leading the community out of the age of witchcraft.

On the prelude of an aborted district conference back in 1998 in Sampwe, there was a youth service out of doors under the trees the night before the district conference was to begin. One pastor told me the attendance count was 900. I doubt it was that many, but there were so many that the church couldn't hold the crowd. Besides great choirs, the youth are famous for bringing dramas into worship, especially a huge youth gathering like this one. They brought a great drama to this one.

The drama was about a family of three: father, mother, child. The child was ill. The father and the mother argued over where to take their ill child. Should they take her to the clinic or to the witch doctor? (I use the term *witch doctor* because that is the term used by the community and in this drama.) The parent arguing for the witch doctor won first, so they took her to him. I was fascinated by the detail shown in acting out this visit. The witch doctor was painted and masked, waving sticks decorated in feathers and offering magic potions and incantations. I also noted the respect (maybe fear?) shown to him by the parents. Everyone in the crowd knew exactly what goes on in a visit to the witch doctor. There was a bit of nervous humor, but no ridicule. At the end of the visit, though, the child was still sick. Traditional medicine could not heal the child.

Then the parents took the child to the clinic. Here the Western doctor appeared in a white lab coat, shades, and a cowboy hat. There was little detail in the scene, but there was a lot of laughter and ridicule. And once again the child was not healed. Western medicine could not heal the child.

The parents finally took the child to church, where she was healed. Here is where the actors in the play lost their focus, and the ending of the drama was mostly chaos. Other actors and youth from the audience tried to fix the ending with suggestions and jumping into the play. The needed result was that the child would be healed at church, but there was much disagreement over how that was to be done. The adult pastor in charge had to call the drama to an end.

At first I thought, "That was a shame. The play was going so well until the disaster of an ending." Then I realized that the ending proved the point. A drama can be a code.

The generative theme is "our children are dying." Coming as a drama from the youth makes the message stronger: "We are dying." Neither traditional healing nor Western medicine is stopping the dying. This fact is common knowledge. The youth, the children, are throwing the problem back at the adults and the church: "We are dying. We are looking to the church to save us."

I marveled at what perfect Freirian code this was, one of the best examples of the process in action. The answer was weak, but a code doesn't present an answer. The youth were demonstrating the tension between traditional healing and modern medicine and finding neither working for them. This is a powerful code. This is how a code works. It is not an answer. It is the reflection of the question back to the community for the community to find an answer. They brought their complaint to the church. This may not be what they thought they were doing, but this is exactly what they were doing. In many ways the church has created this problem and the church has to solve it.

The knowledge of the natural medicines that traditional healers know is being lost as the generations die off. Modern medicines have not come fast enough and in enough volume to replace the traditional ways. The Western medical model may not be the best model.

Another thought: Bishop Ntambo was on his way to replace his grandfather as the village witch doctor. Instead he became a United Methodist pastor. I wonder how much traditional knowledge has been lost because the ones who would have been traditional healers became Christian pastors?

## Kabondo Dianda to Bukama

From Kabondo Dianda, the road goes north to Kamina, an even 100 kilometers, or south to Bukama. We head south.

The hospitality of a full meal takes three hours from our riding day. We are going to be late to Bukama. Then it starts to rain. The road becomes muddy and difficult. The pace slows and we aren't going to make Bukama by dark. In the dark, in the pouring rain, at the intersection of the road and the railroad track, we stop at a restaurant.

Here's the thing about restaurants in these remote places. They're not like truck stops with motels and diners. They are low, grass-roofed, open-air shelters. Women there will cook for you, if you bring the food. That's what makes them restaurants.

We negotiate for tent space under the grass roof. A couple of other men are there, with their mosquito nets hung over their bamboo bedrolls. The roof is not perfect and water is running in small streams along the hard dirt floor, but it is as dry a shelter as one can hope for.

The women heat us some water for coffee and we break out what biscuits (shortbread cookies) we have left. As a rule, I drink only bottled water or water I have filtered myself, but for coffee, anything heated over a charcoal fire works just fine.

This is the ride at its worst and at its best. It's dark now; rain pouring down, grass shelter deflecting most of it, but not all; hot tin cup of coffee made from packets of Nescafe, powdered milk, and sugar; soaked to the bone; good friends. All of my friends are Congolese. I mention that because I sometimes forget and I wouldn't want you to forget that. I live in their world. This is the norm for them. For me, it is exotic and fascinating.

There are two worlds that I'm discovering here. There's the village life, a stable community system. It has plenty of problems: hunger, disease, and permanent poverty. But it is stable.

Then there's the life on the road. It is amazing how many people are living on the road. It takes weeks, even months, to get to your destination. That's a long time on the road. Most are men, but not all. There are also whole families and single women with babies on the road. Some are hitching rides on top of the giant transports, other riding or pushing bicycles, many walking.

Along the way, we have set up our own camp or have accepted the hospitality of a local church, but throwing in with fellow travelers in this restaurant is total immersion in the culture of the road. Jack Kerouac would be proud.

We're up before the sun to get back on the road and make up some lost time. We'd like to get to Bukama before noon. Yesterday's rain has made the road one long mudhole. We ride for a while, then have to stop and clean the mud out of the fenders. I'm not convinced that the fenders are a good idea. It seems to me that flinging mud up my back is a small price to pay for freedom.

Bukama is a river port town and a rail head. From the east, you come upon it from a high ridge that overlooks the town. The descent into town is long and rocky. I have to get off and walk my bike. Bicycles loaded with fish, charcoal, and 55-gallon barrels of gasoline are being pushed up the hill by teams of riders.

It's at Bukama we first hear the rumors of bad news. The bridge at Buyofwe is out. We can get to Luena, but not to Lubudi. This is a problem. I think that possibly there is a pirogue crossing the river there that we can use. Maybe we can use the railroad bridge. There must be one close to the road bridge. But here is where my discipline of not asking questions and trusting the local leadership to solve this problem kicks in.

We ride for Luena.

# *Luena*

*W*e're on our way to Luena. Still no word from Prospère. Shabana is riding with me. He has come from being almost unable to keep up to the strongest rider on the team. He and I have left the team behind and we're riding hard and fast. It's a comfortable fast, just a bit of push in the legs.

My motto is *take what the road gives you.* This afternoon, the road is giving us speed. The road has straightened out, running parallel to the railroad tracks, and it looks flat, but I suspect that it's slightly downhill. The surface is hard-packed red sand, almost gravel. We're hitting 30 kilometers per hour, a speed we haven't seen since the mine road from Tenke to Lwambo. And no traffic is on this road. I realize that it's been weeks since we've seen a truck on the road. Every once in a while, there is a large pool of water in the middle of the road, but that doesn't slow us. It merely breaks up the monotony of a long, straight road. We weave through the chicanes with the grace of Formula One race cars. Hitting the narrow paths just right to negotiate around the puddles reminds us of the speed we're carrying. This is fun.

The day is warm, but not oppressive. We're trying to beat the sun into Luena. It's going to be close.

It's been a few years since I've been in Luena. The last time, I was on the train from Lubumbashi to Kamina, and it broke down in Luena. For twelve hours the train sat in the station. Luena is hot—hotter than hell. I suspect that it's the lower elevation. Locals tell me that it's the heat from the coal mines. I don't know how that works, but there's a lot I don't know about how the world works. What I know is that it's miserably hot in Luena. A couple of local pastors came to greet me and we took a walk around town. I was happy to get off that oven of a train car and walk about. Even a slight breeze or a patch of shade is welcome relief.

The pastors showed me around town highlighting the church's progress and problems. Absolutely nothing was said about the missionaries who used to live here. When we walked past the house that I recognized as the one I had stayed in back in 1991, when I was traveling with a group from Indiana visiting Lowell and Claudia Wertz, they confirmed my recognition but did not take it as an opportunity to tell me about the missionaries who lived and worked in Luena. In September of

1991, just days after we had visited, the missionaries in Luena were evacuated under gunfire, as government soldiers went on a killing and looting spree. Those were the days of terror and heroism for the missionaries and church leaders. For some reason, however, the missionaries and the church leaders do not have a shared story to tell me.

Back in the present, Shabana and I are met at the spur in the road that takes us into Luena by the district lay leader and a pastor, who guide us through the outskirts of town along narrow dirt streets and across the railroad tracks on a bicycle path. We've beaten the sun, but not by much. By the time we get to the main part of town, it is getting dark and visibility for me is below my comfort level for riding, but we ride on.

The streets of Luena are hard-packed dirt bounded by old and broken colonial-era concrete drainage ditches. We ride through a small collection of shops selling cell phone units, gasoline in plastic bottles, and a colorful variety of sundries. The evenings bring out the life of the community. The street is crowded with people, making the ride more socially challenging. Entering Luena is nothing like entering a small village. No crowds of cheering greeters—just a lot of people on the street who ignore your existence.

The host superintendent busies himself with giving orders for our hospitality. It seems he is inventing it on the fly. We wait for the rest of the team to catch up.

We are eventually taken to a walled and gated compound on a large corner lot. An old colonial house now occupied by the Congolese doctor of the mining company, the place displays the awkwardness of a European-designed home now occupied by a semiwealthy African family. To the uninitiated Westerner, the whole picture makes no sense. The yard is mostly dirt. A few plants evidence some attempt at landscaping, but it's pretty lame. A couple of broken-down trucks stand in the drive. Young men with vague job descriptions hang out. Goats and chickens and ducks mill around. Inside, the great room is furnished with a new matching over-stuffed sofa and chairs set facing a large-screen TV. A football match is on. Luena has electricity, and this house has satellite TV. A fan in the corner is moving the air, but the house is naturally cool by design with its high ceilings and thick brick walls.

We're offered a choice of Coke or Fanta. I take the Fanta. (I go back and forth on this option. Some days, I could kill for a Coke. Some days, a Fanta sounds so refreshing. Today is a Fanta day.) Peanuts are served. We sit and watch TV. A bit of football (soccer) and a bit of national news. I realize that I haven't seen TV in weeks and that I've not missed it.

Meanwhile, the back of the house is busy with food preparation, and an hour later, a full African feast is served. The meal that is served to important guests: chicken, goat, fish, even some beef, *bukari,* palm sauce, greens. There are a few table options for the *mzungu:* bottled water, rice, french fries.

We never meet our host. He may be out of town. This seems typical. The church goes to the only member capable of this level of hospitality and asks if he can host a meal.

After the meal, we're taken a few blocks away to what the locals call the Pilot's House in reference to Gaston, the pilot. There is no local reference to missionary John Enright, who built this house in the 1990s. It has a wraparound veranda and, to me, a kind of Australian outback look to it. It sits in a large lot surrounded by a 9-foot wall. A disabled tractor is in the front yard, and airplane pieces are in the back. Gaston lives in Lubumbashi, and I doubt that he spends any time here. A caretaker, a member of the bishop's extended family, and his family live in the small apartments attached to the house. No one lives in the house. It is cleaned out and made ready for us to spend the night. I get the master bedroom. The rest of the team gets the room across the hall.

There's a king-size bed with a mosquito net in the master bedroom. The mattress is like new, and the sheets are clean. There's no running water, but there are a working commode and a shower stall. By *working,* I mean that if you have a bucket of water, they work. I'm brought a bucketful for flushing and a bucket of hot water for washing. This is comfort. The house is wired for electricity, but there is none right now. It comes and goes at the whim of the local utility agency. I suspect someone needs to call them to tell the agency that there is someone in the house. It would be nice to have some electricity to recharge our laptops and my Nook. We've tried getting on the Internet, but no joy.

*I*n the morning, we have a good breakfast of coffee and bread. It takes until early afternoon to arrange a tour of Luena. We walk rather than bike. That's fine with me. I need to stretch my legs.

Our first stop is the United Methodist clinic. If I hadn't already seen clinics in much worse shape, I'd be horrified by what I'm seeing. The little hospital looks as if it had been bombed during the war. It wasn't, but it is in the chaos of construction. The clean half of the ward is curtained off from the dirty half. Three mothers with their newborns are lying on the worn and stained mattresses on antique metal hospital beds. They're not offended by our visit—quite the opposite, they smile when greeted. They look so tired, though. Exhaustion from malnutrition seems to be the leading symptom of life here. Everybody would be a whole lot healthier if they could get a proper meal.

Across from this new ward is the tiny clinic office. Here is the pharmacy and consultation room, along with administration. A woman in here is receiving a blood transfusion. A large sign with the United Methodist Cross and Flame logo on the outside gives the times when the clinic is open. Patients wait out of doors.

This clinic has just received a large grant from the General Board of Global Ministries (GBGM), hence the construction of a new wing. However, its dreams of expansion are much bigger than the grant. I talk with the doctor. He's one of those Lubumbashi-trained Congolese doctors who are among the best and brightest doing amazing things with little financial support. I want to help him, but even with all he needs, he's got much more support than anyone else I've seen. Two things are clear. First, if The United Methodist Church wants to eliminate killer diseases in the Congo, no one has a better network of clinics already in place. Second, it's going to cost billions, not millions, to do it. The need is far, far greater than anyone can imagine. On the other hand, it burns me to know that the Congolese government has more than enough money to build a first-rate, village-based health care system, but it is not doing it.

The problems of the clinic are only a brief distraction from our transportation problem. The bridge is out at Buyofwe. Right now we're dealing with incomplete information, as we don't know if there is a work-around. Don't know much of anything, except that the bridge is out. The church leadership is busy trying to find a solution because if we can't cross the river at Buyofwe, we can't get back to Tenke.

Back in the old days, we could have negotiated a ride on the freight train, but nowadays, foreigners are not allowed to ride the freight trains, and this new law is strictly enforced. I wonder what disaster created that law. In 2008, Taylor and I got stuck in Lubudi, and the church leaders negotiated a place for us in the cab of the freight train, a four-hour ride smashed against the windscreen, in the pitch dark, midnight to 4 a.m.

The district superintendent has spoken with the railroad director. They are willing to add a passenger car to the next southbound merchandise (freight) train just for us, so we have a car to ourselves heading south. We wait at the Pilot's House for word of the train's impending departure. I'm a bit anxious. No, I'm really anxious. I think we should be down at the station, just in case. This is a challenge to my commitment to trust my welfare fully to the church leadership. This is getting to the part of the trip where I have to be thinking about making my flight in Lusaka.

We wait.

First, they come for our bicycles. They are taken to the train to be loaded onto a boxcar carrying motorcycles and bicycles and an odd assortment of cargo. We walk along to be sure they get loaded and because walking is better than waiting. I get really pissed at Shabana as he takes a Magic Marker and writes his name on my leather saddle. I'm under no illusion that my new bike is going to escape cosmetic damage thrown into this baggage hold, but he didn't have to use a Magic Marker on my saddle, and his name to boot. Just when I was getting to really enjoy riding with him, Shabana pulls this stunt.

My relationship with Shabana seems to be my canary in the mine. When I run out of patience with him, I know that I've reached my limit. And I have. I've reached the limit of my capacity to allow other people to control my life. But I've got to play this out. We're still days from Tenke and uncertain if the plan we're on now is going to work.

We go back to the house and wait. It gets dark. About nine o'clock someone comes to get us and hurries us along because the train is loading. I wonder why this person is so anxious because we have a car reserved for us. At the station, in the dark, we find that the reserved car, the one put on the train just for us, is full to overflowing with people. It looks like the stereotype of a train car in the developing world—packed with humanity, and bags of grain, and chickens. All the cabins are taken. All the floor space in the hallways is claimed. We can't even get on. The yelling begins and a cabin is cleared of its occupants. We climb over several families to get into our space, being careful not to step on the babies.

Our cabin is half a Pullman, and there are four of us: Mulongo, Shabana, Éléphant, and me. There's one upper bunk and one lower bunk. The floor is taken by bags of manioc. Our bags take up the rest of the cubic feet of the room. There's a non-functioning lavatory that doubles as a dining table. These old train cars were brought up from South Africa after they had been exhausted in service there. At one time, they must have been nice.

The ambient temperature is north of 100 degrees, hundreds of people in the train car generate additional heat, and even with the window open, the air does not move. My fever is back, and I'm burning up. I get out the first aid kit and tend to the wound on my leg. It's the end of the trail for the team, so there's no need to ration medical supplies. I pass around the kit and others tend to their aches and pains. All of the meds are consumed.

The upper bunk is pulled down and I'm given this coveted location. I protest a bit, but not too much. My bags are on one end, so there's not enough room to stretch out. I roll up my jacket to make a pillow and lay my head down. I'm not just burning up; I'm sweating buckets. My T-shirt is soaked through. I couldn't be wetter if I had just come out of the river.

This is like the Native American sweat lodge I experienced a couple years ago—unbelievable heat, sweating out all the old toxins, getting spiritual crazy. The difference is that the sweat lodge was done under supervision and with an exit to safety just a few feet away. Here there is no one monitoring my temperature or anywhere to go if I feel I've had enough. I'm in the middle of Africa, on a crowded train, running a fever, and there is nothing I can do to change my fate, and yet, I'm at peace. This is the definition of this trip: suffering with those who suffer. There is no safety net, yet I feel secure. I don't think that I'm going to die. I had malaria once and thought then that I was going to die, hoped that I could die. No, this time it is just the fever that is driving all the stuff out of my body through my sweat. It feels good, in a painful sort of way. Or am I beginning to hallucinate?

It's not until midnight that the train begins to move, and even then it moves only a few yards down the track. Then moves back the other way hooking on another car, I guess. This goes on two or three more times until sometime in the next day, we actually move out of the station. We had been on the train for a full twelve hours before we left the station.

I had come to the conclusion that the train never would get moving toward Lubudi and am awoken out of a brain-dead state when it does move. Maybe I was asleep, half asleep, or in a self-induced coma. But we are finally moving now, on our way to Tenke. There is nothing now to do but go along for the ride.

It is night again by the time we reach Lubudi. Having waited at the train station all day for our arrival, most of the church had given up and gone home, but the district superintendent, the pastor, and a few faithful had remained. They have food for us—bread, Fantas, and coffee. That hits the spot. They don't understand why we can't get off the train and come for a visit to the church. Their disappointment does its best to shame us into getting off, but if we had gotten off, there would have been no way to get back on and we'd be stuck in Lubudi. Not a bad place to be stuck, but no. A firm no. Sorry. We had passed the broken-down bridge, but no one on the team is willing to restart the bike ride to Tenke. No amount of shaming is going to get us off the train. The whole Lubudi District would have to hate us for the moment.

Next stop: Tenke.

# *Finished*

The odometer on my bicycle shows that we are just a few kilometers short of 1,000. The next day we ride out to a village to round off the numbers and to get one last visit in. The journey is done and I can set my mind on spring break. I disconnect my inner self from the Congo. The bus ride from Tenke to Lubumbashi is the first leg of the long trip home. I'm going home.

# *Home*

*W*hen I get home, the fever I had in Luena comes back. Unsure if it is related to the sores on my leg or if it is malaria but hating to go to the doctor, I am determined to ride out this fever. However, Teri persuades me that I need to have this sorted out before we head for Fort Myers Beach on her spring break. So I go.

After an unbelievable diagnosis of Baghdad Boils from the infected sand flea bites on my leg, the doctor gives me a prescription for antibiotics.

Teri's question: "Do we have to worry about going into the water with that open sore on his leg?"

Doctor: "No problem."

My question: "What about beer?"

Doctor: "No problem." So, Doc prescribes antibiotics and a week of drinking beer on the beach. I am completely satisfied with the outcome.

The real problem is that I am silent in my decompressing state. It might seem that I would have a lot to say, and on the airplane ride home, my mind is racing with all the stories and learnings that I have to share, but even with Teri, I can't talk. Especially with Teri, I can't talk. It has been months since I've spoken to anyone in English. More accurately, it has been months since I've spoken with anyone who understands English at the same level as I speak it. I know that I had not actually been speaking in other languages, but I had been listening so hard to people speaking in other languages. I had spent months not speaking, just listening. While I want a rolling start at telling everyone what I had seen and heard and learned, I have nothing to say.

We drive down to Fort Myers Beach with friends and spend a week on the beach at our mom-and-pop vacation motel unit with kitchen, right on the beach. Perfect. We spend the days walking on the beach and reading. For fun beach reading, I love Carl Hiaasen. There's no one funnier.

On the beach I finish the draft of what I think will be a book. It is a rework of my Doctor of Ministry thesis, *Scripture as a Tool of Community Development.* I am trying hard to make a totally unreadable manuscript readable.

And I start planning next year's trip.

I'm ready to launch from Mulongo up to Kabalo, into the war zone, to get to Pastor Jackie. But we're going to need a boat.

# *2015*

*I*n the years between the riding and the writing, much has happened and many things have changed. Two things I want the reader to know:

First, Mulongo and I came through the village of New Mind, the tiny village where we first pitched our tents, four years after our first adventure and found that it had been burned to the ground by local militia. We wept.

Second, we recently went through the village of Kabenga, the one with the big church, the one where I had declared that the pastor and his family would not survive. The pastor and his family were thriving. The sun was also shining. I was happy to be wrong.

*A*ll reflections along the way are from what is rattling around in my head. In writing the book, I chose to leave them in the raw as I thought them riding, pushing, struggling with the road. Here, however, are a few of the writers who have influenced and confirmed my thinking.

Conrad, Joseph. *Heart of Darkness.* London: Penguin UK, 2007.

Crossan, John Dominic. *The Historical Jesus: The Life of a Mediterranean Jewish Peasant.* New York: Harper Collins, 2010.

Diamond, Jared. *Guns, Germs, and Steel: The Fates of Human Societies.* New York: W. W. Norton & Company, 1999.

Freire, Paulo. *Pedagogy of the Oppressed: 30th Anniversary Edition.* New York: Bloomsbury Publishing USA, 2014.

Glines, Carroll. V. "The Cargo Cults," *Air Force Magazine* 74.1 (January 1991).

Hochschild, Adam. *King Leopold's Ghost: A Story of Greed, Terror, and Heroism in Colonial Africa.* New York: Houghton Mifflin Harcourt, 1999.

Lee, Harper. *To Kill a Mockingbird.* New York: Lippincott, 1960.

Pirsig, Robert M. *Zen and the Art of Motorcycle Maintenance: An Inquiry into Values.* New York: Vintage, 1999.

Senge, Peter M. *The Fifth Discipline: The Art & Practice of the Learning Organization.* New York: Doubleday, 2010.

Turnbull, Colin. *The Forest People.* 1961. London: Penguin Random House UK, 2015.

Walters, Bob. "Scripture as a Tool of Community Development." DMin Thesis, Christian Theological Seminary, 2006.

Worsley, Peter. *The Trumpet Shall Sound: A Study of "Cargo" Cults in Melanesia.* London: MacGibbon & Kee, 1957. Subsequent editions by MacGibbon & Kee, 1968; and Schocken Books, 1968, 1986, & 1987.